Old Lowestoft
Elizabeth and Jason Freeman

7th January 1905, high tide flood. St. John's Church was built in 1853 by Peto.

ISBN 9781840334654

Introduction

Lowestoft has been a farm, an upstart fishing port, a fashionable watering hole, mercantile centre, railway town, beach resort and frontline war zone. It has been called Lothuwistoft, Lowystofth, Leystoft, Lowstofte. Almost uniquely among English towns, it was still commonly known by a name ("Leystoft") different to its modern appellation right up to the 18th century. In the many centuries of Lowestoft's existence the one constant has been the sea.

The parish of Lowestoft began as a collection of small farming settlements on the high land above Lake Lothing, but the people soon turned to the sea as their main source of income and throughout the Middle Ages Lowestoft experienced steady growth, becoming by 1524 the largest and richest town in the region. During this time it had acquired a market (1306), a beautiful church and a set of well-built dwellings along the cliff edge.

Throughout the next 300 years Lowestoft developed as a fishing and trading port, but the most significant changes began in the early 19th century. In 1800, Lowestoft had a population of 2,332. Soon after Lowestoft was linked directly to London and other centres such as Yarmouth, by the turnpike road (today's A12). By 1871 the population had increased to 13,623, due to the development of the inner harbour in the 1830s, the railway from Norwich reaching Lowestoft in 1847, a more direct line to London via Ipswich opening in 1859 and the building of the outer harbour in 1848.

During the second half of the 19th century the herring fishing and related support industries expanded greatly, so that by 1911 the population stood at 37,886. The town benefited from new leisure facilities, a burgeoning tourist economy and a network of trams. By the outbreak of World War One Lowestoft's layout was broadly as it is today.

Fishing, and especially the herring, has brought great wealth, population and at times rapid change. The sea has meant Lowestoft has hardly been insular, but has welcomed incomers from all places – French, Icelanders, Dutch, and Scots – and has served as a market place for goods and ideas of all sorts. Since the 18th century, bathing has been a popular pastime, bringing holiday makers first in their bathing carts to the Denes, and latterly to the guest houses, promenade and piers of the South Beach. The development of a deep water harbour and the coming of the railway brought Lowestoft, for a time, close to the centre of economic life in the UK, as millions of herring were landed and then transported to London and many other major cities. Throughout its life, the people of Lowestoft have held strong religious beliefs, with Evangelical Christianity giving rise to several "revivals" among the town and fisher folk. These interweaving themes were embodied in the life and work of one man, Sir Samuel Morton Peto, who can rightly be called the father of modern Lowestoft. A committed Christian, and a fair and compassionate employer, he built the harbour, the railway and most of the South Beach sea front. However, he did not only build in bricks, but also sought to construct a spiritual edifice by educating his workforce in the Christian faith.

The golden years of Lowestoft started with Peto's work and ran perhaps until the 1920s. The First World War brought great sadness and fear, and put Lowestoft right on the front line, as a naval port and base for armed fishing smacks. There was great heroism and humour, but things were changing. With the end of the war a new era began. Today the fishing is greatly reduced, and work is scarce. Many of the old industries have closed. Old families have moved away, and many new people have moved in. The authors are no exception: our ancestors have lived in Lowestoft and the immediate area since the 1500s, but today we live in London. However, our enthusiasm for Lowestoft stems from holidays spent there since childhood and the pictures featured in this book are mainly drawn from our personal collection. We hope that wherever you are from, you will enjoy the pictures, and be excited by the history of this part of the Sunrise Coast.

Acknowledgements

Our thanks to the staff of the Lowestoft Record Office who have untiringly [although I know we wore them out] run around gathering documents, and helping in our research. To David Butcher for his guidance and correction. Grateful thanks to Paul Durbidge for his input, advice and loan of photographs and his drawings. To Robert Porter who has so generously shared his post card collection and willingly allowed us to select whatever we needed. To Paul Meadez who always shared his knowledge and willingly aided our research, and proof read the first draft. To the staff of the Royal Naval Patrol Service Lowestoft. To the staff of the Lowestoft Maritime Museum. To Frank Wernham for his kind information and material about the tramway. To David Andrews for loaning a letter from his collection about the Zeppelin raids. To Colin Dixon, who thought he would have a quiet afternoon researching, but found I was there, for expounding to me the ins and outs of motor boat engines. To our friend Joe Beckett for his constant encouragement and assistance in this project. To Wilfred Sutton, Iris Porter, John Swan, Avis and Arthur Bailey for anecdotes. To Emma Clemens for her kind assistance arranging for me to study in Somerleyton Hall and to Lord Somerleyton for allowing me this privilege. To all the photographers whose skill and artistry form the basis of this work. To Richard Stenlake for selecting the pictures and agreeing to publish this book, his grandfather, Frank Douglas Holder, features on page 88. Without the above people this book might never have been produced.

The name Lowestoft is first recorded in the Domesday Book (1086) as *Lothuwistoft*, at that time a small hamlet centred around St. Margaret's Church, and nearby the even smaller hamlet of *Akethorpe*. *Lothuwistoft* means the homestead of Hlothver, who was a Dane. It was not an independent estate, but part of the royal estate of Gorleston.

In 1086, three families (who were not allowed to leave) lived in *Lothuwistoft* as well as ten smallholders and three slaves. They kept eleven pigs, 160 sheep and eight cattle, as well as ploughing the land. There was some woodland and five acres of meadow. Being quite far from the sea, fishing does not appear to have been a major source of income, since Lowestoft did not pay any of its rent in herring, as some places did.

The town stands in the half-hundred of Lothingland, which is virtually an island surrounded by the River Waveney, Lake Lothing and the sea. The half-hundreds of Mutford and Lothingland were at one time a single hundred (possibly called Lothing Hundred). A hundred was the name given to an administrative unit used by the Anglo-Saxon kingdoms from around the 8th century, representing the land which could support perhaps 100 extended families on their farms. At this time Lowestoft was probably one of these farms, sited near the present St. Margaret's Church, which was first established, probably in the 8th or 9th century, as the church for the farm. The main settlement in Lothingland was Gorleston, which at the time of the Domesday Book had twenty freemen (a sign of an old estate centre), and rights over other villages.

Akethorpe, the area to the north-west of St. Margaret's Church, was the farm of a priest called Aelmer, who had three families tending the land for him. It had become part of Lowestoft parish by the fourteenth century, but remained a distinct estate and for many years was owned by Magdalen College, Oxford. At this time Lothingland had for 200 years been part of the Scandinavian world and many of the inhabitants had Danish names, relatives and habits. To the north, the isles of Flegg were entirely occupied by Danish farmers, while Lothingland had been partitioned into estates owned by Danes who forced the English peasants to work for them. After 200 years of occupation the distinctions were disappearing, but 1066 brought a new race of landlords, speaking Norman French and using different names.

In the 13th century, a time of population growth when arable land was becoming scarce, many settlements began to move, as people started to build houses next to greens and commons where they could graze their cattle or sheep. The sea was perhaps the ultimate "common", from which anyone with a boat and a net could earn a living. The cliff side, close to the Denes, became dotted with houses, linked by what has become the High Street, while St. Margaret's eventually stood lonely in its fields.

St. Margaret's Church is a testament to the wealth of medieval Lowestoft. It was enlarged in the 14th century (from when the present tower in Decorated style survives), and the bulk of the church was again rebuilt, in a fine Perpendicular style, in the 15th century. This picture of St. Margaret's dates from around 1911.

The notice is advertising an organ recital by Mr. Ernest Banks, who was born in Norwich in 1869 as the son of a woollen draper, William Banks. By 1901, both had come to live in Lowestoft. He successfully auditioned for the job as organist, and also privately taught organ, piano, singing and music theory.

ST. MARGARETS' CHURCH. LOWESTOFT

ST MARGARET'S CHURCH, LOWESTOFT

The beautiful Perpendicular interior of the church. Many of the leading families of Lowestoft were buried here. With the removal of the town to the sea, St. Margaret's became isolated and suffered structural decay. From 1539 the tithes and land rents that could have been spent on its upkeep were devoted to private uses, while the town's people tended to use a chapel on the cliff top. Reverend Tanner bought the tithes back in 1721 and was able to carry out some internal improvements, but the south wall became unsafe, having to be entirely rebuilt when the church was restored in 1871, at a time when there was great growth in Christian activity and worship throughout Lowestoft.

Beneath the cliffs, the Denes as possibly the safest spot in the Middle Ages between Yarmouth and Kessingland to draw up boats out of the reach of the waves, encouraged families to move to Lowestoft. This picture gives a good idea of the layout of Lowestoft as seen from the Denes circa 1900. The buildings along the skyline to the left were the big houses of the town's merchants and traders, with the High Light just right of centre. The cliffs had been developed as "hanging gardens", while the Denes were not just a dry harbour, but a place to work and live. The buildings on the flat, which was susceptible to flooding, were mostly industrial, net and boat stores and smoke houses. Poorer workers lived on the Denes, in what was known as the Beach Village and some houses can be seen on the far right and left. Most of the houses were demolished some time after the flood of 1953.

As the cliff settlement established itself, the "Scores" which had been formed by surface water draining down the cliffs were developed as little tracks enabling easy access to the beach, alongside which the fishermen and merchants built store sheds, warehouses and workshops, or grew plants in their "hanging gardens". The Scores which remain today are The Ravine, Cart Score, Lighthouse Score, Mariner's Score, Crown Score, Martin's Score, Rant Score, Wilde's Score, Maltster's Score, Spurgeon's Score, and Herring Fishery Score. The photo the right is Maltster's Score and shows a typical scene on the Beach Village circa 1900, with children playing in the score, and washing hanging out to dry in the yards of the row of little houses on the left. Beyond the houses are some industrial buildings to do with fishing, and on the horizon there is the gas works. The single brick crinkle crankle wall (right) is peculiar to East Suffolk and was both cheep to build and strong.

In 1327 England was at war with the Scots. Like all the other settlements of the land, *Lowystofth* and *Akethorpe* had to pay tax to fund this war. Each household had to pay one twentieth of its moveable wealth, unless they had goods of less than five shillings. The records show that Lowestoft's 29 householders together paid £1 9s 6d. This was a comparatively small amount, given that Gorleston (at that time still the main settlement in Lothingland) paid £7 6s 10d., Kessingland £4 2s, and Pakefield/Kirkley £2 1s 3d. It was an average farming village with evidence also of some seagoing, in the personal name Petro le Channdeler. Throughout the 14th and 15th century, Lowestoft grew. It obtained a charter for a market which was held on a Wednesday, and two fairs a year, held on 12th May and 10th October. The market may originally have been on the site of the present town hall, but it later moved to the Triangle near the High Street.

The Market Place, next to the Black Swan beer house, in Old Market Plain. At the time of the photo, in the late 19th century, the Black Swan was owned by Messrs. Youngman & Preston, and from 1904 was run by Harry Alladay Hartley who took over the licence from Emmanuel Harmer.

Like several Suffolk villages, Corton was once much bigger in the Middle Ages, and wealthy. In 1327 it was "worth" £2 2s 6d., almost two times the value of Lowestoft, and had eleven inhabitants paying more than one shilling in tax whereas Lowestoft had only one such inhabitant. However, by 1524 it paid only £2 18s in tax, as against Lowestoft's £35, and had just one inhabitant paying more than £1. Such villages simply could not compete with the fishing ports. It was from this time that intense rivalry with Yarmouth blew up. The burgesses of that city, jealous of their fishing and trading rights, insisted that no fish be landed within seven miles of the city unless they received a tax. For many years the dispute simmered on, occasionally erupting into violence until it was eventually resolved in the 1600s, in Lowestoft's favour.

Corton Church Ruins

In 1524 when Henry VIII was at war with France and Spain, each person had to pay a tax on lands and goods. There were 163 taxpayers recorded in "Leystoft" who together paid £35 18s 7d Lowestoft was now the largest and richest town in Lothingland, far surpassing Gorleston (the next biggest village), which had 48 taxpayers who paid £5 9s 8d Most other villages paid £1 or £2 or less. In Mutford hundred, the villages were generally richer, Kessingland paying £9, Kirkley £5, Pakefield £3 and the inland villages only £1. The source of the wealth at Lowestoft seems to have been the sea. There were a variety of foreign taxpayers in Lowestoft and the other fishing settlements, such as Bernard Frenchman, John Rabue Frencheman, Jamys Ducheman, Petyr Ducheman and William Marshall Scottyshman. Fishing and trade brought these people to the Suffolk coast. In 1568, two Icelandic boys are recorded serving in "Lowstofte" inns, a fact which recalls the long fishing journeys made by Suffolk boats to the frozen north since at least the 15th century. Records show that boats from Dunwich were fishing off Iceland in the 15th century.

A typical wealthy Lowestoft townsman of the time was William Colby (an ancestor of the authors) who, in 1534, left his fishing boat to his son John, the owner of several other fishing boats. He had a warehouse with salt, fishing boats and tackling, but was not just a fisherman as he also left cattle and farmhouses.

YE OLDE SWANNE LEYSTOFFE

There were many wealthy people in Lowestoft who could afford to build houses of brick. This pen and ink sketch, by local archaeologist Paul Durbidge, shows a cellar under one of the buildings in the High Street. It was constructed some time in the 1400s, possibly as a private chapel, or simply as a room for storage. The quality of the brickwork shows that there was plenty of money concentrated in the owner's hands. Above this cellar once stood Ye Olde Swanne, where Oliver Cromwell stayed in 1643 when he came to Lowestoft to suppress the supposed Royalist uprising there, suggesting it was one of the best Lowestoft dwellings of that time.

Flint House, High Street, Lowestoft

An example of a Lowestoft dwelling of this period is the Flint House. Above the door the initials "WM" stand for William and Mary Wilde, with 1586 the year they built their house at the top of Wilde's Score. The score was probably their own access route to their property on the beach. The Wildes were a local family who were on the ascendant. In 1524 Wylliam Wylde (the original spelling of the name), owned £2 worth of goods, but by 1568 there were three Wildes namely William senior (£8 goods), Roger (£6 goods) and William junior (£3 goods). The last-named is possibly the William who lived here. By 1640 John Wylde was one of the richest taxpayers in Lowestoft. When the monumental brasses in St. Margaret's Church were removed by Jessup, it was Joshua Wilde who bought them as scrap. Bells which were made from the scrap were hung in the Town House. An epitaph to the family in St. Margaret's Church reads: *Here resteth the body of John Wilde, eldest son of James Wilde, the youngest son of John Wilde, the eldest son of William Wilde, the only son of William Wilde, all merchants of this town, and are buried in this church of Lowestoft 1700.* In 1788 Wilde's School, provided for by the will of another John Wilde, opened behind the house, for 40 boys to be taught to read, write, do accounts and learn Latin. The school's motto was: *Train up a child in the way he should go and when he is old he will not depart from it.*

Wilde's Score

Recent excavations, by Paul Durbidge, beneath the John Wilde School, during building work, produced numbers of clay pipes, clay marbles, pottery and animal bone, along with fragments of painted plaster. Outside there was much evidence of dumping during the post-medieval period. The later excavations of the adjacent drying area were highly productive, with remains of imported salt glazed bellamines (a sort of bottle), and the blue and grey Westerwald Jugs, being recovered near exposed cobble spreads, the drying area was where people dried their linen and clothes in the 17th century. They also dumped their rubbish down the Scores. There was further evidence of trade, from German jettons, tin glazed earthenwares, and fragments of North Italian marbled ware. Medieval remains were found at depth and included a copper alloy chape circa 1250-1540 and a pronged buckle. A number of soot-blackened pot sherds found with animal bones close by in burnt sand, were of 14th century date, and these included part strap handles from jugs.

The 17th century was an eventful one for Lowestoft. Throughout East Anglia there was religious controversy between High Anglicans and Calvinists. During the Civil War, a group of Royalists came to Lowestoft and tried to seize the town for the King (a useful port, since Yarmouth supported Parliament), taking guns from the Batteries to point inland. They sited them, at the top of Rant Score (pictured below).

However, Cromwell arrived and disarmed them without a shot being fired. He also took the Rector of St. Margaret's, Rev. Rouse, off to Cambridge Gaol, a reminder of how close were religion and politics in those years. This picture looks north up the high street towards the town hall built by Peto (the Italianate tower in the distance). Before this on the left is the Crown Hotel. E Lacon & Co. Ltd. brewers is on the right, at the corner of Rant Score.

During the Commonwealth, the Calvinist dissenters were able to found a church in 1655, with support from clergy from Great Yarmouth. They held meetings in a barn in Blue Anchor Lane (now Duke's Head Sreet), the road leading off on the left of the picture on page 7. More joined the church when non-conformist clergy were ejected from their parishes in 1662, following the Restoration of the Monarchy. This was in many ways an underground church, meeting in members' houses and sharing communion in Yarmouth until 1689, when William and Mary passed the Act of Toleration. A chapel was built in the high street in 1695.

In 1603 Lowestoft's population was around 1,000 and by the beginning of the 19th century, within a three mile radius, it had increased to 2,332, far surpassing the surrounding settlements. By 1860 the population had increased to around 10,000. As the census shows, there had been a great influx of builders, surveyors, architects, accountants, bankers and doctors into Lowestoft and the proprietors of hotels and business employers were nearly always people who had been born elsewhere. Between these dates, Lowestoft had become a fashionable bathing resort, where ladies and gentlemen could stroll on the Denes and benefit from the sea air and water. However, the population growth was built not on tourism, but on Lowestoft's maritime character, and the industries that grew from that. Herring and sea trade had been the mainstay of Lowestoft for centuries, with good and bad years. The *Ipswich Journal* of 1st Nov 1777 stated: *The herring fishing this year at Lowestoft and Yarmouth is bad indeed. What with rivals in the north, multitudes of dogs, and stormy weather, the merchants are almost frightened out of the trade.*

To keep the boats at sea, much work was needed on land. A major industry in Lowestoft was manufacturing the ropes and nets needed for fishing. The rope was made out of hemp, which was locally grown in the "hemplands," (where a street still bears that name). As the fishing fleet grew, the hemp had to be imported from the Baltic. It was made into rope by hand on the Denes near Lighthouse Score, whilst most of the net making work was done by people at home.

Messrs. Beetons Ltd., of the Beach Village, were many years of this trade. Women net makers, called beetsters, made all kinds of nets, trawl, herring, agricultural and others. The nets were made by hand until the 1960s when machines started to be used as well, but a lot of the work was still done by women at home.

In the 1950s every drifter used about 90 nets, which stretched for a total of over two miles when in use, giving some idea of the amount of netting required. Nets were put overnight into hot tanning baths. The solution, which was made from the bark of the acacia catechu tree, preserved them and gave them a distinctive colour. The nets were then hung out to dry on the Denes, before having corks fitted.

Fishing was not the only industry practised in Lowestoft. A directory for 1793 lists other manufactories in the town as china wear and ropemaking. Hewling Luson discovered suitable clay on his Gunton property to produce good quality porcelain and in 1757 he opened the Lowestoft China Factory in Crown Street (later known as Factory Street) which was in operation until 1802.

This porcelain shows traditional Chinese designs. The bowl bears the bridge design, and the small dishes are floral. The decorative painting was mainly done by women, who worked upstairs in the attic where it was light. In 1784 Maximilien de Lazowski visited the factory, whilst on a tour of England as a guardian and tutor to two French brothers. He wrote in his journal that the factory produced china for everyday use and that 90 to 100 workers were employed and that there were two kilns using only coal as fuel. The fire was kept burning for 28 hours to bake the china and then the china was left in the kiln for three days, to allow time for it to cool slowly. While a skilled worker earned fourteen shillings a week and apprentices seven or eight shillings a week, some painters commanded salaries of a guinea or a guinea and a half a week. However, the china was made for the general market, blue and white cups being only threepence each and those with gold borders, sixpence. One reason why this factory was built at Lowestoft was because of the foreign links that already existed. Lazowski noted that about half the china was exported to Holland and, from there, to France where it was sold as Porcelain des Indes.

On 11th October 1764 John Wesley preached at Martin's (then known as Gowings) Score inthe open air. It is likely that many present were fisher folk from the Beach Village, and this was the beginning of a religious awakening. A Wesleyan society was subsequently formed. The first Methodist church was built in Friary Lane, and opened by John Wesley on 19th November 1776. There was also a Primitive Methodist Chapel in Denny's Score, which opened in 1827. In 1803 premises were obtained in Bell Lane and in 1862 the Free Methodist church was built in London Road North.

Because Lowestoft was so far from the parish church, there was a chapel of ease in the town. Evening services were held in the town hall, but when the 400 seats were taken it was full, so many people went to the Primitive Methodists in Denny's Score.

In 1830, the evangelical vicar, Rev. F Cunningham, became Rector of St. Margaret's Lowestoft. He oversaw the building of St. Peter's Chapel in 1832 which seated 1263. Marriages were not conducted there, but continued at St. Margaret's. Rev Cunningham gave 36 years service to Lowestoft, and 42 years to Pakefield. For 26 of those years he was vicar in both parishes and his home was open day and night to people. His wife was Richenda Gurney, who was the sister of Elizabeth Fry , an early prison reformer.

ST. PETER'S CHURCH, LOWESTOFT.

Looking towards the sea, the town of Lowestoft formed a T shape, with the down stroke extending inland. A map of 1831 shows the town lying along the High Street, which at its extremities becomes the "North End" and the "South End" respectively. The High Street follows the curve of the cliff (which can be seen in the picture below), but the roads leading beyond the "Ends" are dead straight, reflecting their origin as 18th century turnpike roads.

In this late 19th century picture where the man is standing, on the left outside No.160, is Howard Bunn "Naturalist fish, bird and animal preserver". He also sold tobacco and cigars. Next door, at No.162, was C. E. Nobbs the grocer who advertised Fry's chocolate and Cocoa in his window. A little further down on the same side was Woodcrow, watch and clock maker. On the right of the picture at No.31 is A.H. Hinde, Dispensing Chemist. Most of the buildings, however, are dwellings. The houses on the High Street were, by the time of the 1841 census, mainly occupied by professional and wealthier people. Interspersed amongst them were shops. However, the sewage here was rudimentary until after 1847 when a drainage system was installed. This helped prevent outbreaks of malaria, which previously had been common in the Waveney region.

In 1852 the peace and serenity of this street scene was rudely disturbed when the newly erected plate glass front of Devereux Bros. grocery establishment narrowly escaped complete smashing by a runaway horse and cart. The horse started at Oulton and ran two miles to Lowestoft, rounding corners successfully before entering Crown Street, which it passed down at speed. When it reached the corner of High Street, Vincent (the postman's pony) and his cart were standing against the pavement kerb, leaving a space of not quite seven feet between themselves and the Devereux shop front. As it rounded the head of Vincent's pony it passed between the cart and the shop front without touching the former, and merely leaving a slight graze of the shaft upon the north and a patch of grease off the hub of the wheel on the south door pillar. The horse continued down High Street and the London Road, and was ultimately stopped at the bridge, after a run of nearly four miles, without doing any other damage.

Bayfield and Cullen, butcher and dairy shop, was built on the site of Ye Olde Swanne. They also supplied meat wholesale from a shop in Battery Green Road and ran a bakers in Suffolk Road. In the picture the staff of 1920 are standing outside the butchers shop. On the left side, in the doorway, is Amy Campbell, who was chief cashier. According to Amy there was a cellar, under the shop, which had ancient arches. People thought there was a tunnel from it that led to St. Margaret's Church, but no evidence has been found of this. Paul Durbidge has pointed out, that if it had existed it would have been discovered when the railway cutting was made for the railway line construction from Lowestoft Central to Yarmouth South Town.

This shop looked over the sea, at the back, as did the old wealthy merchant houses. One of these houses went up for sale in 1819 and was described as: *A desirable and spacious residence, eligibly situate in the centre of the High Street. A mansion house, with coach house and stables, all necessary attached and detached offices, in an excellent state of repair, the eastern front fitted with bow windows, and commanding an extensive view of the ocean. A large hanging or terrace garden of near an acre, walled in, and well planted with choice fruit trees and a vinery. At the foot of the garden there was a neat dwelling house, fish offices complete and capable of curing 70 lasts of herrings at one time, also a tan office, with vats and a large copper, for the tanning of nets and ropes. The mansion house comprises a capacious arched cellar, two kitchens, a servant's hall, a breakfast parlour, dining and two drawing rooms of large dimensions five good sized bed rooms and three attics.*

Flanking the town, facing out to sea, were two batteries, the northern lying in what is now Belle Vue Park, and the southern at Battery Green. These were gun emplacements, probably first installed by Henry VIII and maintained throughout the next three centuries to protect the town from such enemies as the Spanish, Dutch and French. Queen Elizabeth I presented Lowestoft with four pieces of ordnance and two slings. However, the cannon were not always used for defence, being plundered during Kett's rebellion to batter the walls of Yarmouth, as well as being seized by Oliver Cromwell when he captured Lowestoft. The batteries marked the edge of the town, and aside from a few large houses along what is now London Road North and a plot of dwellings at South End, there were no buildings south of St. Peter's Street.

This is "South End" looking up Old Nelson Street towards the High Street around 1900. The grass in the foreground is part of Battery Green. Old Nelson Street led down to the South Battery and the beach before the turnpike was built. The building with the small square towers in the centre of the picture is the former Congregational Church.

Although men had beached their boats on the Denes for many centuries, this could be risky due to high tides and flooding. Larger ships had to be anchored in the open sea and were exposed to storms. Lake Lothing was separated from the sea by just a spit of land, which occasionally flooded. Heading south from Lowestoft travellers had to pass over dykes abounding with shrimps. If this spit could be breached, boats would be able to pass safely into Lake Lothing, and from there into the Broads and the Waveney. They could therefore get to Beccles and Norwich without sailing all the way up through Yarmouth. To this end in 1814 work was begun by the Norwich and Lowestoft Navigation Company (who in 1825 to 1828 had to raise further funds by issuing more shares at £100 a share) and it was completed in 1831, with a sea lock and swing bridge at Lowestoft, and the improved Mutford Lock at Oulton Broad. When the fresh water met the sea, hundreds of fresh water fish died, and were found floating on the surface of the lake. They were carried out to sea on the receding tide, and were found later on the beach having been bitten by dog fish.

The mud that was dredged up was taken off, in 1829 and 1830, and used to make up an embankment at Mutford Bridge, and to build up the shores of Lake Lothing at Oulton Broad. It seems that one of the last tasks was to create the "New Cut" from Oulton Broad through to the River Waveney. The newspapers of 1829 mention that the route was staked out with fences across the marshes, and people were warned that removal or damage of these would result in prosecution.

At this time, the main mode of transporting goods around the country was by water. Wherry boats were used to move goods through the broads, such as cut reeds for thatching and later, after Swonnels Maltings were built, to transport barley through the Broads.

At the start of 1831, construction of buildings began at the harbour mouth itself. Tenders were invited to build: *an engine and boiler house, for two steam engines, a dwelling house, with office and board room adjoining, and a carpenter's and smiths shop and coal stores.*

However, by the summer of 1831 there was public concern that Mutford Lock would be too small and not be able to take boats of 100 to 120 tons. Mr. Cubitt addressed these concerns at the annual assembly of proprietors of the Norwich and Lowestoft Navigation Company, quoting other similar navigations in Scotland and in Canada. He said that the depth of water at low tide would be twelve feet, and twenty feet at high tide at Mutford Lock, whereas the Welland Ship Canal in Canada was only eight feet deep and 22 feet wide and was for vessels of 120 to150 tons, whilst the Aire and Calder Navigation's locks were only nineteen feet wide and seven feet deep but could accommodate vessels carrying nearly 100 tons. The size and depth of water at the Lowestoft sluice would be 50 feet wide and water depth twelve feet at low tide, and twenty feet at high tide. These dimensions, he said, were amply sufficient for the largest class of steam vessels and for any sailing vessels that could navigate the Lowestoft Roads.

Mr. Bennett, in support, said that he had had many conversations with captains of vessels that would use Lake Lothing as a harbour of refuge. Recently there had been more than 300 vessels driven in the roads from Yarmouth, and he claimed that it would produce a much greater income, as a harbour of refuge, than was at first contemplated.

The New Cut was an opportunity for a certain group of enterprisers, and in April 1832, soon after it was opened, the first known case of smuggling occurred. Near Mutford Lock a large 42 foot galley was boarded by coastguard officers who found about 200 items of foreign brandy and tobacco on board which they then seized and deposited in the Custom House. The crew managed to escape, however. This event caused new concerns about the opening of the navigation system, as revenue would be lost unless officers remained alert. This is a picture of such a galley in Lake Lothing.

In 1831 money began to run out, £89,000 already having been spent. A new Act of Parliament was needed if further money was to be raised. The sea lock gates had been damaged by the teredo worm penetrating them, and the tide kept blocking the entrance to the inner harbour with sand. It became impossible to sluice out the entrance with water from Lake Lothing, and the channel silted up. Income dropped because shipping declined, as the new larger ships could not navigate the waterways. The reduced income was insufficient to repay borrowed money and as a result in 1835 the company was put up for sale, although it failed to find a buyer.

In 1843 Sir Samuel Morton Peto (1809-1889) came to live in Lowestoft, where he lived at Somerleyton Hall. Not only did he develop this Jacobean building into a modern Victorian mansion, but he also built much of south Lowestoft between 1847 and 1862. This gave Lowestoft a new look and changed it forever. The former rector of Somerleyton, Rev. Edward Brooks, said of this Victorian entrepreneur: *He proceeded to turn Lowestoft from a small fishing village into one of the main ports of the country, with a new harbour for 1,000 ships and some luxurious hotels for the growing holiday trade. He also built the railway connecting Lowestoft to the rest of the railway system, thus fulfilling his promise that fish landed in the early catches would get through to Manchester in time for high tea.*

While the New Cut was not as successful as had been hoped at its outset, at least the swing bridge at Lowestoft lasted fairly well, and kept the feet of travellers dry. It was made of cast iron and was opened manually several times a day to allow the passage of boats through between the inner and outer harbour. This photo shows the original bridge before it was replaced in 1897 and was probably taken in the early 1890s.

The inner harbour in Lake Lothing enabled more and bigger boats to be used off Lowestoft, and so trade and fishing developed between 1830 and 1850 as did related industries, such as net manufacture, rope making, fish selling and handling, sail making and shipbuilding. Although the Norwich and Lowestoft Navigation Company had failed, the new harbour development was too important for local enterprise to be left standing still. A consortium of Norwich and local businessmen bought the company for only £4,005. They later sold the harbour to Peto for £12,500, and by an Act of Parliament in 1845 he proceeded to develop the harbour area further.

This picture shows smacks in the outer harbour, facing South Pier, with the pavilion to the left and St. John's Church to the right. The drawback of the inner harbour was that a lock and a bridge impeded access and when sand was washed in front of the gates it was impossible to pass through. Between 1846 and 1848 Peto built the north and south piers which formed a harbour straight out to sea, thus providing an anchorage for vessels and protecting the entrance to the inner harbour from silting up. This encouraged more fishing vessels, and freed up the banks of Lake Lothing for other purposes.

In 1851, The *Artisan* wrote: *The new harbour comprises an area of about 21 acres and consists on the south side of a long straight pier 28 feet in breadth at top, and which runs out to sea nearly a quarter of a mile, being terminated at the extremity by a circular end 60 feet in diameter. In the centre of this straight pier is a lighthouse, and the whole extent of this straight pier is defended by a wooden parapet, and the surface boarded for a footpath, so that it forms an excellent terrace for walking, a privilege which is purchased by subscription, or by a payment of a penny per day at the toll house. The whole of this pier is substantially constructed of massive main piles driven down opposite each other from five to seven feet apart, longitudinally braced together by longitudinal waling pieces and diagonal braces.*

In this photograph a smack is leaving the harbour as a steam drifter prepares to enter. Crowds of pleasure-seekers throng the South Pier, the North Pier contains cranes and other industrial equipment.

This Lowestoft Harbour scene shows a barge tying up. In the background several trawlers are moored in the trawl basin. To the right is LT 7 *Pandora*, built 1885 and lost in collision on 25th January 1911. Her crew, who were all lost, were skipper Sterry, deckhand F. Brady, 2nd hand H. Lincoln, who left a widow with six children, and cook J. Cross, whose body was trawled by another Lowestoft smack two days later. In the centre is LT 502 *Boy Walter*, built in 1909 and sunk by a submarine in 1917.

This picture, taken from the north arm of the yacht basin, shows the fish market as it was in about 1910 with to the far left a glimpse of the houses in Waveney Road and, to the right, the masts of boats in the herring basin. Dredging the harbour mouth remains necessary to this day. The harbour is not a natural river mouth, and tends to silt up in an effort to return to the state it was in as a spit of land. In the 19th century insufficient dredging led several boats to get stuck on the sand which built up, and at low tide people could walk across the harbour mouth.

On 5th December 1896 the *Active* LT 237 was grounded on the sand bank between Lowestoft Harbour piers and was refloated the next day. She was a wooden dandy drifter that had been built that year by Chambers and Colby of Lowestoft. From 1906 to 1911 she belonged to Yarmouth and was renumbered YH 979 before being sold to Norway.

Two other boats were also stranded in the harbour mouth and had to be assisted off the sand that had built up, also on 5th December 1896. They were a trawler LT 517 *Prairie Flower* 1892 to 1911 built by Colby & Chambers and LT 468 a drifter *Girl's Own* 1892 to 1900 built by Richards.

For Lowestoft to prosper, and to compete with Yarmouth, it needed a railway. Peto contracted with Stephenson to build the Eastern Counties Railway, including the railway system from Lowestoft to Norwich. When this opened in 1847, the train engines used coke, which was produced in coke ovens, from coal that was landed on the Lowestoft quay. After 1860 coal was used instead. The Lowestoft Railway Station building was built in 1850. Now that Lowestoft had a port and a railway, fish could quickly be transported to other parts of the country. In 1859 Peto decided that fish would arrive in London faster if it did not have to travel via Norwich, so in 1859 the East Suffolk Railway was opened from Lowestoft to Ipswich. These two railways became part of the Great Eastern Railway in 1862.

Peto had halls built for the railwaymen for their leisure hours and gave them religious and educational books, as he believed that education could reform behaviour and elevate the mind. He also gave every worker a Bible. The gin shops were left deserted, and the schools were full. The good conduct of Peto's railway labourers under his system was exemplary and it is said that not one appeared before the courts on a criminal charge.

This shows the north side of the station along Denmark Road, where the main entrance still is. A lady and a girl can be seen running towards the booking office to catch their train. To their left is the parcel office, where items could be shipped to *England, Ireland and Scotland, and to the Continent.*

With the railway and the harbour, Lowestoft became a flourishing centre, in particular in the trade with Denmark (reflected in the street names Denmark Road, Tonning Street and Flensburg Street). In September 1850, under Peto's influence, cattle began to be imported from Denmark, followed by horses, pigs and sheep. English farmers bought these and were so pleased that the trade increased, and in 1853, 16,000 cattle and 10,000 sheep arrived. Stables were built by the North of Europe Steam Navigation Company on the North Pier in 1852, so that the animals could rest before being sent on by train to London. The August 1852 market report stated that 684 beasts and 425 sheep had arrived at Smithfield Market, London from Tonning in Denmark.

Unfortunately the cattle trade faltered when a cattle illness appeared on the continent and in 1859 the North of Europe Steam Navigation Company collapsed. The cattle sheds and stables were bought by the Eastern Counties Railway, but the cattle trade with the Continent failed entirely when war broke out between Denmark and Prussia and Austria, in 1864.

Today in Lowestoft there are still a few gentlemen, approaching their centenary, who remember bullocks being brought by train to Lowestoft, to make their final walk to the abattoir. As soon as they were spotted being driven in groups by men with sticks, a boy would shout out "Bullocks", any boy who heard him would shout the message on. "Bullocks, bullocks," echoed through the streets of Lowestoft. Doors flew open, and children came pouring out to follow the bullocks up the road. Dogs barked, boys shouted, mothers screamed at the smaller children to come in, and the bullocks, terrified of the smell of blood and noise often stampeded or ran the other way towards the children. Of why the children got so excited, John Swan said: "Have you ever seen a bullock get off a train?". He grew up to become a butcher and worked at the Co-op.

With the harbour and the railway, the focus of Lowestoft shifted decisively from the Denes, towards Lake Lothing. Housing for fishermen and labourers was laid out between St. Peter's Street and Denmark Road so that industry could flourish, but with its golden sands, Peto could see an opportunity to also develop Lowestoft as a leisure port. Tourists had frequented Lowestoft since at least the 18th century. Bathing machines were used on the north beach from 1768, and were available for use from May to November. It was usual to participate in this medical cure by 10 o'clock in the morning. Men would be suitably attired in one piece striped costumes with three quarter length sleeves and legs. By the 1790s, Lowestoft was already a popular watering place. In 1812 there was a bath house on the beach close to the water, and another was opened in 1824. This was a pebbled building with a magnificent view of the coast. Its reading room, decorated with maps, was sufficiently spacious for the holding of balls. There were four baths for hot and cold bathing, a medicated bath and a retiring room to which gentlemen adjourned for coffee and a quiet game of cards. Ladies used it for bring and buys and sales for charities.

Peto bought wasteland which was just south of the bridge and, beside the sea, for £200. On it he built the Esplanade, which was a continuous line of semi-detached villas for wealthy owners, and the Royal Hotel which was opened in 1849 at the north end (on the right of this picture) for elite visitors. Marine Parade was completed by him in 1851. These houses overlooked the well-kept gardens at the back of the Esplanade, but were considered to be second-rate holiday accommodation.

Wellington Terrace, which also overlooked gardens, was finished in 1856. During the summer a class of people, described in the advertisements as "superior", occupied residences in these properties. Many houses were let fully furnished to families who were accompanied by their servants. Others were divided into suites of self-catering apartments that accommodated up to eight people. They were advertised as fashionable properties with sea views, and views of the windmill in Mill Road. Many also had stabling for horses.

The south basin of the harbour was set aside for yachts and other water sports. The effect of these developments can be seen in the depiction of Lowestoft in Trollope's *The Way We Live Now* (published in 1875). Paul Montague and Mrs Hurtle choose Lowestoft rather than Cromer, since *there is a railway all the distance*, and there was plenty to do with *shipwrecks every other day*, although the Royal Hotel was *a small little place of only a hundred beds* (chapter 42). It was *the long strand which made Lowestoft what it is*, to which people flocked in August and September.

The South Pier, opened in 1848 as part of Peto's harbour development, became a popular promenade, especially with visitors. Peto placed a square reading room on it in 1854 where gentlemen could go to read the newspapers (in the centre of the picture), and there was a telescope so tourists could examine the passing shipping. This picture, taken before the yacht club was opened in the 1880s, gives an idea of how the wasteland along the coast looked before South Lowestoft was developed.

The centrepiece of Peto's tourist town was the Royal Hotel. During 1852 The *Lowestoft Journal* carried an announcement stating that the proprietor, Sam Howett, had, during the winter, provided extensive suites of bedrooms, in addition to the wing constructed the previous summer and that this would prevent a recurrence of those disappointments which so frequently took place from his inability to accommodate his 'friends' in the past year. It was his intention also to persevere in that course which had already given such general satisfaction viz to combine the best wines, viands, attendance, and cleanliness, with moderate charges, ease of access and lowness of fares every Wednesday and Saturday.

The 1875 town guide spoke of the Royal Hotel as situated at the northern extremity of one of the noblest esplanades in the United Kingdom, an entirely new and handsome building, which offered first class accommodation to travellers of the highest rank. One of these was King George V who dined with some of his naval officers when he visited the naval base during the First World War. The hotel was requisitioned by the Admiralty for five years during the Second World War and was demolished in 1973 after years of debate.

Peto was a deeply Christian man, and wanted to ensure that residents and visitors in South Lowestoft were provided with spiritual care, a need also recognised by others. Writing in 1847, Suckling in his *History of Suffolk*, commented, *Some peculiar circumstances connected with the town, make a new provision for public worship absolutely necessary. In the bathing season the church [probably St Peter's Chapel] is not sufficiently large for the congregation, and then it would be expedient to open a second place of worship. With the harbour and navigation extensions, for the persons attendant upon this harbour, the church is most inconveniently situated.*

So in 1854 St. John's Church was opened to cater for South Lowestoft, at a cost of £7,500, paid by Peto. The architect, John Louth Clemence, later became a mayor of Lowestoft, and the builders were the Lucas brothers. This is a view of St. John's Church from the Royal Plain. The fountain, erected in memory of Lowestoft's last Lord of the Manor by his cousin, Mrs Mary Ethelrind Franey, and around which the children are congregating, was later moved to Kensington Gardens. The clock was put in later, in 1887, by public subscription to commemorate Queen Victoria's golden jubilee. Unfortunately the stone selected for this building began to deteriorate, and as it was going to cost £5,000 to restore it the church was pulled down instead in 1977.

Peto encouraged, supported and financed many other significant Christian evangelical activities in Lowestoft. The Chapel for Seamen in Commercial Road and the Missioners' Home were also part of Peto's development plan.

Peto married his cousin, but she died in 1842, leaving him with three daughters and one son. In 1843 he remarried and moved to Norwich and then to Somerleyton, where he built a Baptist church in the grounds of his estate to cater for his tenants.

Peto was a Baptist, and when he came to Lowestoft, he and his wife attended the Old Meeting House and burial ground in High Street. John Dovery, of Middlesex the minister had a young lady friend of whom he was extremely fond and whom he desired, but she chose someone else. Supposedly the shock made him go white overnight. Peto and Dovery were united in an understanding of what it was like to lose someone they truly loved and this was possibly the factor that drew them together in a fine friendship. Rev. Dovery eventually did marry.

In 1852, Peto built a new Baptist building called the Arcade Chapel, using plans drawn up by his architect Clements. Too small with leaky roof skylights, and buildings either side that blocked out the light this site was sold in 1894.

Peto changed Lowestoft from a fishing village into a port and tourist town. He was Lord of the Manor, M.P. for Norwich from 1847 to 1855, carried out international contracts, and built a railway in the Crimea for the army in 1855 (for which he was made baronet). He was involved in the building of the Houses of Parliament. In his dealings with employees he was moral and caring, but he was bankrupted in 1886, following a bank collapse and died three years later.

Although Peto clearly hoped to make a profit from his investment in Lowestoft, he did not aim solely at making money. Soon after his arrival, he engaged and paid the missionary William Johnson to look after the spiritual needs of the harbour and railway workers. Johnson was a missionary with the British and Foreign Sailors' Society, which was inter-denominational, and had been formed in London in 1833 with the aim of the *moral and religious improvement of seamen*. It rapidly became international with a branch in all major British ports, and abroad.

When in Norwich Peto frequently attended the Rev. Wm. Brock's chapel, and Rev. Brock joined Peto in his plans to benefit the navvies on the Eastern Counties Railway. Peto opened a railway mission account, at the Norwich Bank, upon which Mr. Brock had liberty to draw. One day Peto bumped into the Bishop of Norwich at the railway station. The bishop drew Peto to one side and said to him: *I cannot part without expressing to you as the Bishop of this diocese, the great obligation you have laid me under in your care of the spiritual interest of the poor men on the line. I have anxiously watched all that has been done, and I can assure you all has my most sincere approbation and approval.* Later Peto said that he felt the liberality and Christian feeling which dictated the remark, as he was conscious they differed on what many esteemed questions of importance. The bishop had said that Peto was a dissenter, and that he envied the sect to which he belonged the possession of such a man, he would gladly purchase him at his own price and heartily prayed that he would ere long become a member of the Church of England. [cited from Sir Morton Peto – A Memorial Sketch for private circulation]

Johnson held meetings in beach sheds at first, then in railway goods sheds and upstairs over the Customs' House between 1850 and 1854. In 1864, Peto built the Chapel for Seamen in Commercial Road and the Missioners' Home adjoining. Out of Johnson's work grew the Sailors' and Fishermen's Bethel, which was built in Battery Green Road.

Johnson's work was very effective in the Beach Village, where many fishermen lived. What had been a scattering of houses in the early 1800s had grown to a population of 2,500 by the First World War. Many of the inhabitants were affected by the evangelical preaching of the time and all the churches built on the beach were evangelical.

In 1859, a religious Revival began to sweep through the UK, in which people listening to preachers felt a deep awareness of their wrong behaviour, and at the same time a great gratitude to

God for forgiving them. In 1861 this Revival arrived at Lowestoft, when two evangelists named Reg Radcliff and Henry Schouldham preached at Lowestoft Town Hall and 500 people were converted and added to the church, many of whom were fishermen. In order to cater for the many new believers on the beach, Christ Church, known as Cunningham Beach Memorial Anglican Church, was founded in 1869. There was a lot of zeal and activity at Christ Church. Bible classes, day and Sunday school, temperance meetings and mid week services were held as well as open air meetings down on the beach and on the fish market. It was around this time also, in 1871, that St. Margaret's Church was restored.

The Christian work in Lowestoft focused especially on fishermen. The orange sailed Lowestoft vessels looked magnificent as they sailed off into the distance, many to be away at sea for eight weeks, and only home for six or seven days. In 1881 London, alone, was supplied with 194,000 tons of fish from the North Sea. The fishermen wore heavy boots, large baggy trousers and layers of flannels, pullovers, and waterproofs, even on a hot day. Living conditions were cramped and the cabin was a small, dark hole. Long hours were full of hard toil, battling against wild weather to earn a crust of bread and struggling through storms, snow and frost, during black winter nights with howling wind. The grey sea was a foaming wilderness swept by pitiless wind, often like the hand of death. It was a hard life.

The Thames Church Mission believed that these men deserved better things to improve their lives at sea and so in 1882 they sent a smack named The *Ensign*, to be used as a Mission vessel to cruise with the fleet that was close to Gorleston and Lowestoft. It was under the command of a fisherman who was an agent of the British and Foreign Bible Society, the Church of England Temperance Society, The Shipwrecked Mariner's Society, and the Thames Church Mission. This smack carried a library, a harmonium and also a medical chest.

Many fishing boats drew up alongside the *Ensign* and many fishermen rowed over to the Mission ship and boarded her. Fishermen lounged on her deck, and then went below where they packed into every corner, and available space, to hear the Gospel and Bible being taught, and to sing hymns, the melody of their singing filling the air and floating across the ocean.

A former secretary to the Thames Church Mission, Ebenezer Mather, founded the Royal National Mission To Deep Sea Fishermen, which was established in Lowestoft in the 1890s, in Suffolk Road. They also had a mission smack that sailed with the fishermen for their six week voyage. She flew the mission flag and would anchor on Sundays amidst the encircling fleet, to hold services. One of the last mission smacks was the *Sir William Archibald*, which made her last voyage out of Lowestoft just before the Second World War. After about 70 years at sea the RNMDS moved onto land.

From 1902, the Rector of St. Margaret's was the Reverend Tupper-Carey, known as "Tupper", who spent much of his time ministering to Lowestoft's fishermen. He held special services for them at church, and even went to give them words of encouragement when they were away fishing in Cornwall and the Shetlands. He was frequently on the fish market, boarding boats and chatting affably with the men, and was often to be seen, in top hat and clerical coat, riding home on his bicycle with a large handkerchief full of fish, dangling from the bars, waving and greeting people as he went.

This picture of Corton Parish Church gives an idea of the services held for fishermen. It is decorated with fishing nets, floats and baskets for the Harvest of the Sea service on Fishermen's Sunday, when thanks was given to God and prayers said for "those in peril on the sea". During Tupper Carey's incumbency, the Roman Hill Mission took off. Originally the congregation met in homes, then in a marquee, before building a wooden shed. In 1902 Tupper-Carey borrowed £500 to pay for a corrugated iron structure, St. Andrew's Church, which lasted until 1933, when a more permanent structure was built. After eight years, Tupper's ministry at Lowestoft came to an end. The Archbishop of York wrote that he wanted to appoint a canon, *whose main duty would be to arouse a new sense of the interest, the romance, the obligation of the missionary work of the church. What I had heard of my old friend Tupper's labours for the cause at Lowestoft turned my thoughts to him.* So in 1910 Tupper accepted the invitation to become a Missionary Canon of York Minster.

Around 1900, many other evangelical Christian movements came to Lowestoft. The Salvation Army Band was active at open air meetings in Lowestoft as well as leading rousing hymns in the citadel. In October 1896 General Booth came to Lowestoft and preached to a packed meeting in the Public Hall. The seating had been rearranged to accommodate the large gathering of mostly uniformed Salvationists who had come from various places including Ipswich, Norwich, and Lowestoft. Booth preached

YWCA LOWESTOFT.

for an hour, the title of his address being, "The Salvation of the Salvation Army." He said: *I find most Christian people a deal more miserable than worldly people, because the latter have no concern for eternity. There are many who think the Czar a very important person, in fact he fills a far larger place in their horizon than does Almighty God.*

He emphasised that once having accepted the salvation offered to them so freely, men should live up to it, and show to the world the force of the principles they professed to have accepted. He referred to the indifference existing among such a large number of people about their eternal welfare, and how difficult it was to get them to realise the magnitude of the offer made to them. General Booth in drawing to a close reminded everyone: *To obtain this gift you must give yourselves up entirely to God, and then claim what He promised. Then your sins will be completely blotted out never to be brought up against you.* Two years later, in June 1898, the 600 seat Salvation Army citadel in Whapload Road started to be built, funds having been raised through Citadel Company shares.

The new Young Womens Christian Association began in Lowestoft in 1885, but this home was opened at Lowestoft in 1897, by Mrs. Garratt (wife of Canon Garratt), as a boarding house for working girls who went to Lowestoft for work but who could not find accommodation. It was built at the lower corner of Regent Road, at a cost of £1,729, Mr. Clarke being the architect and Brett & Son the builders. YWCA homes were advertised as homes where girls would be lovingly seen after, and where they would receive spiritual instruction in the various classes, and find recreation in secular entertainments. The matron was Florence Emily Herrmann, aged 28, who had worked as a governess in Sussex.

In 1912 Lowestoft hosted the National Evangelical Free Churches Conference. Delegates who had booked were listed in the local newspaper. The three day conference was held at the Hippodrome and the paper carried an outline of all the sermons.

Baptist Church, Lowestoft

Christian faith and work remained a major part of Lowestoft life throughout the early decades of the 1900s, and it was at the London Road Baptist church (on part of Grove Estate, where Boots is now) that Lowestoft's third religious revival began in 1921. To the right of the church in this picture is a plot of the Grove Estate still for sale.

Douglas Brown was the son of Archibald Brown, who was the Minister of East London Tabernacle Baptist Church. He went to Lowestoft in 1921 to preach for a week, but stayed on for several more. He preached without fee or reward and addressed 310 meetings, where over 1,000 people were converted. The Scottish fishermen who attended those meetings took the revival with them back to the coastal towns and villages of Aberdeenshire.

Mr Greasly was the port missionary. He ran Bible studies at the Bethel for some of the young people who became Christians during the revival. In the second row from front is Amy Campbell fourth from right, and here sister Nora fourth from left. Years later, Amy recalled that in the 1920s, the Bethel was so full that fishermen sat on the window sills, and you had to be there early if you wanted to get a seat.

Lowestoft's population continued to grow steadily from 1801 to 1851, but then doubled to 13,623 in 1871 and had nearly trebled again to 37,886 by 1911. With its extensive harbour facilities and other transport connections, seagoing activities flourished. The fleet grew from 30 vessels in 1801 to 80 luggers in 1841. By 1871 there were 210 vessels, and in 1891, 700 in total, including 300 trawlers. Lowestoft fishing boats were drifters and trawlers. Herring and mackerel, being surface fish, were caught with drift nets. Fish such as cod, whiting, turbot, sole, haddock and plaice were deep sea fish and had to be trawled.

At the opening of the 19th century, herring drifters had three masts with large square sails, called luggers by Lowestoft men. The numbers of these craft increased in Lowestoft from 1840 to 1850, although by the middle of the century many boats had two masts, so there was more room for bringing the nets in. In the 1860s fishing trawlers, from Ramsgate, came to fish off Lowestoft, and trawlers soon became popular with Lowestoft fishermen.

LT 438 smack 1891-1908 *Chanticleer* is seen here leaving the trawl basin, just raising its topsail. Once out at sea, the crew raised more sails fore and aft. These ships were steered just by a rudder, which sometimes took two men to manoeuvre. When the crew were actually fishing the rudder was lashed in place. *Chanticleer* was eventually lost in collision 7th February 1908.

LT 669 *Sunbeam* was built by boat builders Chambers of Lowestoft in 1905 and was sold to Sweden in 1937. Here it can be seen in the trawler basin moored end on. This made unloading the catch more difficult, but enabled more ships to dock. The main sail is neatly rolled. Not all skippers were as thorough at the end of a trip, but the best ones ensured the equipment was put away properly.

In the spring Lowestoft smacks spent four months fishing off Padstow, Cornwall, for sole, but the sailing drifters followed the herring shoals up to the west of Scotland in the summer and back down the east coast to Lowestoft in the autumn. It was during the 1860s that fishing boats from Fife began to appear for the herring, and by the 1890s boats were coming each year from all along the east coast of Scotland. By the 1880s to 1890s the boats were larger, with ketch-rigged sails, so could carry more nets and consequently catch more fish. They also had steam-powered winches to haul in the nets. These were the boom years of the east coast fishing, and Lowestoft's harbour grew with it. The Waveney Dock extension was made in 1882, and in 1892 the basin was improved for the trawlers. In 1902-1903, Hamilton Dock was built to accommodate all the Scottish boats, because there were so many.

To the left of this picture, can be seen the fish market, built in 1872 by the Great Eastern Railway Company, who owned the harbour. The tower was a lookout tower, where someone would not only check for ships in distress, but also see which ships were coming in first. At ground level fire buckets were hung on the tower.

The smacks are moored in the trawler basin side to side, so that the crew on the left would have to clamber over three other boats to get ashore. Such were the crowded conditions of the harbour then. To get in and out of the harbour, the smacks had to wait for the wind or the tide, and when the tide went out or the wind blew eastward, the boats would sail out as a fleet. This was an impressive site, which people crowded onto the South Pier to watch.

Likewise, on the return trip, the smacks often lined up at sea to await favourable conditions. Each skipper hoped to be the first home in order to get the best price for his catch, which would be shared between the boat owner and the crew. After the owner, the skipper got the prime catch, followed by the mate and last of all, the cook. Wives were known to send their sons down to watch for their husband's ship to return in order to secure the catch before it was shared with any friends in the pub.

In 1833, a story goes that one Lowestoft fishing boat caught a very large cod nine leagues eastward off the coast of Lowestoft. The ship's master, Robert Gowing, decided that the fish should be prepared at sea ready for sale in the market the following day. The cod's belly was so huge that it was cut open and to everyone's astonishment a new born baby boy was found inside. It could not have been in there long for it was still perfectly formed, but not alive of course.

Smacks returning to Lowestoft Harbour, one of them the LT 74 *Star of Peace*. When there was a good breeze the sailing boats went faster which caused more pull on the trawl, and this resulted in a better catch of fish. Older people still recall the beauty of the familiar red sails against the sky as they watched the fishing smacks sail by. These sailing boats, however, were being replaced by steam engine boats. This photo was taken in the early 20th century and a Lowestoft tram can be seen crossing the bridge.

The more extravagant skippers might use a tug to get out of the harbour when there were contrary winds. This was fairly expensive, so as in this picture several smacks would share the cost. You can see that at least two boats are following the tug *Imperial*, linked by tow ropes.

There were two paddle steamers, *Imperial* and *Tribes*, which were used as working tugs. *Tribes* is the front tug here, with the other tug towing a sailing ship into the harbour.

In 1897 Lowestoft had her first steam drifter and by the early 1900s steam was the mainstay of the fleet. Such vessels could fish further, and in harsher weather, than the sailing boats, and they held more fish. The introduction of the steam drifter led to a boom in herring fishing.

This is the *Lord Charles Beresford*, LT 1046, built in 1907 at Selby (she foundered in 1926) seen leaving the harbour, with a crew of at least seven, not all of whom were necessarily fishermen. Skippers frequently took their sons or friends along for the trip in the school holidays. Old sea dogs recollect that the first day was always an exciting adventure, but was soon followed by sea sickness, and many wished they had never gone. Wilfred Sutton, one of those lads recalled: *The young-uns had to keep clear of the activity when the cry "Up trawl" rang out, and when the "cod end" was hoisted up the mizzen mast, swaying and dripping, and full of marine fish, crabs and sea weed, the lads were allowed sternwards. The cod end was pulled from the base of the net and the catch flopped, smacked and crashed onto the deck. Crabs and lobsters crawled for shelter, small whiting wriggled, and plaice tried to turn over to camouflage themselves. This was exciting. While all this activity was in progress the smack was in full sail. When they used to shoot the trawl at night the school boys had to keep below, in semi darkness. It was so easy to trip or fall with so many ropes on the deck, and also the lads would have got in the way.*

A Fraserburgh boat racing to catch up the returning drifter *Friendly Star* LT 370, which was built in 1909 and was broken up after stranding in 1941. There were often near misses as boats raced back to be the first to sell their catch. In the distance on the left is a smack with all its sails unfurled.

LT 473 drifter *Myrtle Sprig* built in 1910, sold to Great Yarmouth in 1923 then broken up 1935.

The steam drifter was itself eventually replaced by diesel trawlers. LT 347 Ala class trawler was a prototype of an order for twelve North Sea trawlers in 1934, fitted with Ruston diesels. It was designed and built at Lowestoft by Richards Ironworks. At the time of their completion they were the largest group of fishing vessels with standardised oil engine propulsion in Europe.

LT 337 was a diesel fishing boat that was operating during the 1960s. Wilfred reminiscing said: *No sailing trawlers now, instead huge diesel driven trawlers, with fish holds large enough to contain a bungalow! Dragging and scouring the sea beds, with huge iron chains and nylon nets, but better conditions for the crew though with proper toilet conditions and cabins. The sailing smack toilets were the scuppers for a wee, and a small wooden barrel to sit on for a poo, not below deck, of course, but in the open, with something solid to hang on to in a breeze.*

HERRING DOCK, LOWESTOFT.

The port of Lowestoft during Home Fishing circa 1913 and the Herring Dock crowded with ships, fish boxes and barrels being packed on the quay. Many of these drifters came from Messrs Richards' Yards. This was the golden age for herring fishing. The fish industry was booming and the local papers reported in 1911 and 1912, that there was so much demand for herring, particularly on the continent, that the great herring harvest was employing thousands of men and women at Lowestoft. Such was the local interest that the papers frequently mentioned where the herring shoal was, during the rest of the year, such as off the Shetlands, and where the Lowestoft fleet was fishing when away from home.

It was reported of The Home Fishing voyage of 1913: *The like of such a voyage has never been known in any port in the world.* The number of Scottish herring drifters at Lowestoft and Yarmouth totalled 1163, made up of 854 steam drifters, 100 motor and 209 sailing. Crans of herring landed at Lowestoft numbered 536,400, while crans of herring landed at Great Yarmouth were 823,600. On average there was 1,000 fish in each cran. These averaged £1 a cran, so the value of the catch was £1,500,000.

Fishermen wearing oilskins and boots, unloading herring in baskets in the Trawler Dock, with the South Pier pavilion in the background. Four of these baskets equalled one cran. There were so many fish caught that many were dropped onto the quay. As soon as the boat landed the skipper would take along two or three baskets to the auction area, which were tipped out onto the ground, so that they could be examined by potential buyers of that catch. After the auction, at which the price was agreed with the highest bidder, the whole catch was unloaded onto the quay, and the fishermen were careful not to underfill the baskets because the buyer might be watching. This resulted in filling the baskets to the top and in some fish sliding off. Children hurriedly picked them up, ran a wire through their gills and threaded them on to a wire. Joe Becket said that because he knew a lot of the skippers, they used to let him have fish. He would walk along the lower ledge, between the fishing boats and the market itself, and compete with the seagulls to get them. When his semi-circle of wire was full he walked back home to Oulton Broad to give them to his mother, by which time they had grown very heavy.

A great variety of fish species appeared at the market. Ling, conger eels, cod, skate, plaice, whiting, herring and mackerel lay in piles. Boxes of prime turbot, brill and sole were carefully packed. Occasionally other fish were caught that made the visitor stop and stare, such as dory, wolf-fish, porpoise, halibut, sturgeon or probeagle shark. Heaps of whelks, boxes of oysters, Cromer crabs and heaps of scallops, all waited their turn for auction. The bell clanged and the auctioneer spoke at a tremendously fast rate selling lot after lot to the fish buyers. These purchasers processed their fish for transporting and resale elsewhere. Behind the crowd are the offices of some of the fish merchants who traded from Lowestoft.

The fish market was a noisy, busy place. Bells clanged, boxes banged, lots of shouting and bustle as the fish were speedily taken from the boats, put into boxes, auctioned off and then the place was cleaned up and hosed down and trolleys carted boxes away. Visitors were allowed on the market to view the whole scene, and the seagulls swooped screaming and had their fill. With such quantities of fish being landed at the harbour, a large labour force was required to land and process the catch, and there were many opportunities for business men to make money. One such man was Jimmy Campbell, from Fraserburgh, the son of a sail maker on a Scottish whaling ship. Jimmy became a cooper and made fish barrels, later setting up his own business as a wholesale fish merchant and curer and employing Scots girls to gut and pack the herring he bought into barrels for export to such places as Poland. They travelled round the coast following the herring. This took him to places such as Hull, Lowestoft and the Hebrides.

The picture shows James Burnett Campbell on the trawl market in front of Morton's office. He met a local girl, Amy Maria Hook, and they were married in 1903.

This photo of their wedding includes members of several prominent local fishing families, including the Colbys and Hooks.

Front row are bridesmaids: from left to right are Dorothy Hook, Minnie Hook, Lilly Hook, Hilda Hook and Sissy Hook.

2nd row from front: Maria Hook, Marion Hook, James Burnett Campbell (Groom), Amy Maria Hook (Bride), ?, William Colby (bride's grandfather from Pakefield), Eliza, and William Campbell.

3rd row from front: Fred Hook, Florence Hook, William Hook, Edgar Hook, Daisy Hook, William Hook, Elizabeth Hook, Harry Hook.

Back row: Polly Newson, ?, Harriet Hook, Robert Hook, ?.

Amy moved away from Lowestoft to live in Fraserburgh and then in Hull, but was homesick to return. So in 1917 they came back to Lowestoft and settled in Pakefield at Glen Manna.

A Record Catch, Lowestoft.

Jimmy Campbell (*above*) was a cheerful and popular personality in Lowestoft, particularly in the fish trade. He became large over the years and weighed 22 stone, so was easily recognised and appears on several postcards. This was a bumper catch of herring at Lowestoft at the fish market before being auctioned off. Jimmy is standing with hands in pockets just right of centre.

Left: After the auction the baskets of herring were carried to the troughs for gutting.

A group of herring gutters, at Lowestoft on the Denes, employed by Jimmy Campbell. The barrels are marked "JBC" for James Burnett Campbell. During the busiest times, some of Jimmy's children came to help out, and his son, Bill Campbell was a cooper.

Fishing Industry 'Gutting' Lowestoft. N1808.

The gutting girls worked nimbly and could do this task rapidly, often wearing bandages to protect cut fingers from the stinging salt. They frequently sang as they worked.

Not everyone was willing to host this invasion, but many did. They were glad of the extra money earned by housing them and squeezed the girls into their houses, which were almost full with their own families. The smell of fish clung to their clothes, so much so that some had to leave their garments hanging up in the outhouses.

After work the girls could be seen walking through the streets knitting. People remember the bright coloured wools they used in their Fair Isle patterns, and watching their fingers working at speed.

There were huge numbers of barrels on the Denes as can be seen in this Edwardian photo. Children played in the new empty barrels. One of the happiest boyhood memories of Wilfred Sutton, now a popular local artist is of playing down on the Pickling Plots where Birds' Eye factory is now. This was where most of the Scottish people worked. Wilfred used to play on these barrels with the local boys, running on top of them and kicking the stoppers off. This caused the liquid to shoot up into the air, like fountains, all over their socks. If the policeman didn't catch them when they ran, their mothers did when they got home stinking! *The smell of the new wood was lovely and fresh. Many of the lads were taken, one at a time, for an involuntary roll in one. The pickling plots was a glorious playground, climbing the pyramids of barrels, walking on them and using cast off wooden hoops for making bows and arrows. Hide and seek was popular too with so many barrels around.*

Barrels were laid on their sides and topped up with pickling liquid, made from the juices and blood of the fish, and the bung reinserted. After the herring were gutted they were packed methodically into barrels, each layer being sprinkled with salt and, after the lid was put on, the barrels were left upright for ten days. After this they were reopened and topped up with more fish of the same age before being rolled away and stacked, on the Denes, ready for export. The owner's initials were generally stamped on the barrel lid.

The barrels were taken by cart to the ship for transportation. When the 2nd World War came, Jimmy Campbell, like other merchants, had exported his barrels of fish to Poland, but the money was frozen and he lost out.

This group of people worked in the Beach Village. The men were coopers, and the women in oilskin aprons were fish gutters, whilst the other girls were beatsters who made nets.

The sea and sands off Lowestoft, especially the Newcome Sands and Holm Sands, could be extremely dangerous, and it was easy for boats to run aground and be wrecked, sometimes with great loss of life. To protect the passing shipping, in 1609 Lowestoft was the first place in the country to have a lighthouse erected by Trinity House. This was the Low Light, which stood on the Denes. The light was moveable, so that the High Light and the Low Light could remain in line with the moving Stanford Channel, which altered its position with the variation in the sand banks. Shipping could thus navigate passage to the harbour in safety. In later years the light had to be moved because of the gradual encroachment of the sea. This candle-lit beacon once stood at the bottom of Swan Score, later known as Mariner's Score. By 1779 the Low Light had been moved to the bottom of Spurgeon's Score. Over the next hundred years it was moved many more times. The photo shows Mariner's Score circa 1900, looking down to the Denes and some of the industrial properties there. Beyond them is the Low Light, with a smack sailing past. Mariner's Score is named after Mariner's Inn, which stood at the head of the score. It was previously called the Swan Inn, so the score was also Swan Score. Before this, it was known as Scarle's Score. Local artist Wilfred Sutton recalls happy boyhood memories of this score, particularly the central hand rail.: *We children used to slide down that rail at quite a speed ,without holding ,with legs spread out in front, bumping over the rounded oval joints of the vertical supports. The rail was polished to a silvery shine by our rumps. I remember seeing a young fisher girl's wedding ring in the rail. It got caught in there and no one could ever get it out.*

A Lowestoft sailing boat painted by marine artist George Vemply Burwood (1844-1917) who used to live in Mariner's Score. He was orphaned as a baby and his grandmother brought him up. He started work as a cooper, which gave him the opportunity to chip away at wood to make ship models which he developed into clockwork models. Some of his models won him a medal in exhibition; Princess Alexandra bought one of his models for Queen Victoria. Burwood is one of a group of artists known as the Pierhead Painters ,the others being Jack P. Gregory, Ernest G. Tench, Thompson Swan and George Race. He is best remembered for his beautifully detailed paintings of boats.

He had a large family of children. He also supposedly adopted two children from overseas who were rescued from a shipwreck; the boy grew up to be a clerk and the girl a nurse, but it's not clear whether the story is true.

These are the coastguard and fishermen's cottages in Lighthouse Score, just below the High Lighthouse. The first High Light was erected in 1676, and the last was built in 1874. This light was lit by coal, and was used in conjunction with the Low Light near the Ness. Close by the High Light in the picture is part of the original beacon which was replaced by a 40 foot brick building. The cottages were bought by Lowestoft Corporation in 1897 and have since been demolished.

Such were the dangers at sea that there evolved a kind of code of mutual protection, under which sailors and fishermen would try to help others who got into difficulty. The Lowestoft Beachmen, who spent their working lives at sea and so knew the sands well, were tough and very brave, unsparingly risking their own lives in order to try to save others. They did not always succeed, losing their own lives instead

On 8th January 1838 a foreign schooner got into difficulty, ten miles out to sea, off Lowestoft. There was a high wind and thick driving snow. The schooner hoisted a flag for a pilot to guide them through the dangerous sands. The men on the shore saw the flag, and reckoned that there would be other boats in difficulty too, so at 2 p.m., two yawls set off with their main sails up. The first yawl carried one pilot, and the second yawl, *The Peace*, had two pilots on board, together with its crew of Beachmen. The weather worsened. A high east north east gale blew the thick driving snow, making it impossible for *The Peace* to see ahead.

The first yawl turned back, because they could see that a boat from Yarmouth had reached the schooner to supply a pilot. This yawl got back to Lowestoft, at 7 p.m., with the news that there were no other foreign ships out there, but *The Peace* did not return.

People waited and grew anxious and began to think the worst. All twelve men were indeed drowned and in the calm of daylight only floating hats and wreckage were to be seen. The loss was not only the value of the boat at £170, nor the loss of winter livelihood for the whole Beach village, obtained by using the boat to get anchors and to assist vessels in distress. The real loss was to the twelve widows, some pregnant, and 32 children who were left destitute without a father to provide for them. In total 58 people, who were families of beach men, were left with no means of a livelihood. Money was collected for the widows.

The crew that were lost were:

North Sea pilots: James Cullingham, James Smith
Beachmen: John Rose, James Cook, James Bobbitt, William Capps, Robert Capps
Additional Beachmen: Samuel Gilby, Joseph Saunders Junior, William Saunders, Thomas Cooper, John Liffen.

Above: Here a whole group of people are scavenging what they can from a wreck. Two men can be seen with sacks to gather small items. Not much of the boat is left beyond its keel. What the waves left behind, the Beachmen took away.

Left: The Old Beach Company Beachmen outside their "shod," circa 1900. From left to right they are: Peter Smith, Tom "Brock" Ellis, Sheppy Hook, Dixon Peek (seated), Harris Allerton, and Joe Painter Swan. There were beach companies in many of the coastal villages. These were associations of men who, as well as fishing, would earn money by salvage, taking possession of ships which had been abandoned by their crew. When the captain of a passing vessel accepted that his ship was lost, he would abandon it, and it was often saved by the Beachmen who came out in their boats. His ship would then be theirs. This may explain some of the "trophies" on the front wall of the shed. The figureheads most likely come off large merchantmen, and the names nailed up are those of some of the ships salvaged. The two badges near the apex of the roof are probably the emblems of a trading company whose vessel the company took. The primary aim, however, of going out to save those in peril was humanitarian, and it was out of the Beach Companies that the lifeboats grew.

Left: Robert William Hook (1828-1911) was one of Lowestoft's most famous lifeboat men. Over 6 feet 3 inches tall and strong, he was coxswain of the Lowestoft lifeboats from 1853 to 1883. During those 30 years he saved hundreds of people, also a cat and a dog. He is depicted here wearing his medals. He was awarded an RNLI silver medal for rescuing the crew of the *Shamrock* in November 1859, another silver medal for the November 1872 rescue of the crew of the *Expedite* which was grounded on the Holm Sands off Lowestoft, and the Berthon medal for the rescue of eight men from the *Berthon* which stranded on the Holm Sands in November 1882. Hook lived in the Beach Village, in Denny's Score and Spurgeon's Score, where he was beer house keeper of the Rising Sun and then the Fisherman's Arms.

Right: Thomas "Brock" Ellis (1815 - 1899), was the son of Thomas Ellis, mariner and fisherman, and Elizabeth Capps. He was one of the Lowestoft Beachmen who received medals for lifeboat rescues, and was a Trinity House pilot. The lifeboat was originally kept on the Denes, and launched by the Beachmen, who lived close by. Thomas was a big man, 6 feet 3 inches tall and weighing 22 stone, and was very strong. Jack Rose in his book *The Grit* said that Thomas "Brock" Ellis was ship wrecked in 1835, and swam for seven and a half hours in the sea, before reaching land. *The Times* newspaper gives the story, but calls him Samuel Brock.

The Lowestoft lifeboat trials February 1892, before a crowd of onlookers, with from left to right the yawls *Deal*, *Glasgow* and *Samuel Plimsoll*. The *Samuel Plimsoll* was Lowestoft's lifeboat from 1876 to 1905. She was launched 83 times and saved 165 lives.

The *Stock Exchange*, which was funded by the Stock Exchange, was also used in these trials, but was damaged so badly that the Beachmen refused to man her again. This must have been a blow for their colleague, W.T. Ellis, who built her on the north beach and was paid £373 for her.

This sail lifeboat, the *Kentwell*, served for sixteen years at Lowestoft between 1905 and 1921 and saved 165 lives. Here she is leaving the harbour with a full crew in sou'westers. She was the first to be kept afloat in the harbour, so did not have to be launched each time to go on rescues. The Lowestoft lifeboat is based in the harbour to this day. The smack in the background is LT 84 *Boy Cloud*, 1899 - 1925. The *Kentwell* was replaced by the first motor lifeboat the *Agnes Cross*.

Edward "Ned" ELLIS (1843-1920) with Waverley and Ford Jenkins around 1900. Ned Ellis was a fisherman and lifeboatman whose family had been in the Lowestoft and Kirkley area since the early 1700s, as lifeboatmen, beachmen, fishermen and boat builders. In 1884, after 20 years as a member of the official RNLI lifeboat crew, he was elected second coxswain of the boat, the *Samuel Plimsoll*. In 1885 and 1886 he was appointed to look after the Pakefield No. 1 boat when she was lying in Lowestoft Harbour and in 1886 he became coxswain of the volunteer lifeboat *Caroline Hamilton* until she was taken out of service in 1891.

Such was the great affection that Beachmen could have for a reliable vessel that when the *Caroline Hamilton* was due to be auctioned off, Ned boarded the vessel and refused to leave. He vowed that he would not allow the sale to take place, and that if it did he would chop up his beloved boat. He said that the committee had appointed him coxswain and that he intended to remain until the same committee asked him to resign. A police constable was called who went on board and wrestled with Ned but could not disarm him. After this, Ned calmed down, and the auction went ahead. The knockdown price for the vessel was £80 and the buyer was Mr. Butcher, Ned's uncle. Ned remained quietly on the boat for some hours after the sale. Finally he left voluntarily, having caused no damage. After being used as a vessel for summer trips from the South Pier at Lowestoft the *Caroline Hamilton* was converted to a yacht and then became a houseboat at Beccles. Finally she was broken up at Brundall.

During his life Ned Ellis saved many lives. He and his son Edward received a medal at the Imperial Institute of Yachting and Fisheries Exhibition in London in 1897, amongst other medals and awards, and his lifeboat service is commemorated on his headstone.

Not all ships foundered far out at sea. Many came to grief around the harbour mouth and on the shore line, due to strong winds and accidents. This is the *Fronjot*, a 450 ton Norwegian vessel which had been in Lowestoft with a cargo of timber for Messrs. Saul. On 5th September 1907 she set off on her return to Chrstiania, Norway, towed out of the harbour by a tug. The sea was choppy and the wind was strong, causing the ship to roll heavily. Midway between the South Pier and the Claremont Pier, the tow rope parted, and the *Fronjot* was driven back northwards, where she was caught in the eddy tide outside the harbour and whirled with a terrific crash onto the North Pier. With the seas breaking over the rolling boat and the tall masts quivering, the crew scrambled up the rigging to get onto the pier, which was crowded with onlookers. The ship's back was broken and she was beyond salvage, so the men tried to save what moveable stuff and stores they could. It was an unfortunate trip for Captain Anderson, the commander and owner. He had tried to sell her before leaving Lowestoft, but didn't accept the figure offered. Now she would only be sold at breaking-up price and his loss was great. However, no-one had been killed and in years gone by fishing vessels had been dashed to pieces at the same spot, with great loss of lives.

LT 278 *Moss Rose*, a Lowestoft sailing fishing boat, was built in 1889 and was sold in 1910. Here she is seen in collision and grounded, on 17th March 1903, with the *Semper Fidelus* LT 292. The latter boat, which had been built in 1882, ended her life on this occasion. Here the *Moss Rose* is secured by a cable from the top of her mast to the pier to stop her toppling over. The railway lines and trucks in the foreground are being loaded up, possibly with salvage, while other men are hauling ropes across the beach. Such wrecks attracted sightseers, who here are lining the shore.

In 1898 the *Adana*, which was stranded ashore at Corton in bad weather, took several weeks to be dug out, and several tons of sand were shifted. Here are the digging party posing with some of the bags they filled, before the *Adana* was towed back out to sea (by the cables which can be seen stretching off to the left).

On 9th January 1912 this Lowestoft fishing boat *Mystery* was returning to harbour when she was stranded at the North Pier and was wrecked. Again, plenty of sightseers are crowding the North Pier to watch her demise.

On 26th October 1909 this Fraserburgh sailing drifter FR352 *Daisy Bell* was returning to Lowestoft with her catch. As night fell a storm blew up, and by the early hours of 27th October, it was at its height. She tried to dash to the harbour through the Stanford Channel, with her sail up, when the heavy sea jerked the sail round. Before the crew could lower it, the boat was driven into the roads, across the breakers and onto the beach, just near the Low Light. Fortunately for the crew, George Balls and Arthur Adams from the Gasworks saw the wreck. They called to the fishermen to float a bladder on a rope. George Balls rushed into the sea, tied the rope to a groyne, and both men hauled it in, with the help of Mr. Nichols, the keeper of the Low Light. By the time the coastguardsmen arrived, the crew was saved. The fishermen went to the Sailors' Home, where Mr. and Mrs. Ruthen, the caretakers, made them comfortable. However, the *Daisy Bell* was badly holed and became a complete wreck. Here she has been secured by ropes from her mast while the crew try to save what they can from the ruin.

SS *Longwood* of Glasgow, September 1909. While on a voyage from London to the Tyne she became leaky, and was taken in tow off Lowestoft. She had a big list to starboard, and was almost waterlogged as she was taken into Lowestoft Harbour to be pumped out.

The dangers were not just out at sea. When the seas and winds were rough, Lowestoft could face destructive flooding on land, as storms whipped up the high tides. This was a particular risk to the people of the low lying Beach Village. In this picture the sea is battering the sea wall which protected the Denes, and spreading over the promenade. Such wild seas have at various times caused devastating coastal erosion, and at other times dangerous floods. In January 1905 a high tide caused flooding in Lowestoft. It was the second storm surge in that week and the highest known to that generation. The *Lowestoft Journal* recorded that there was considerable damage in Norfolk and Suffolk and that the Denes houses and streets at Lowestoft were flooded. In its description it stated: *The Beach Village suffered. The gale was blowing from North west, it was high tide, and roller after roller seemed to pile on the top of each other and like a solid mass they dashed on the beach and impelled by the power of the tide mounted the sea wall and spread over the whole area of the Denes…. The spectacle was a magnificent one, but distressing with all, because of the result. The oncoming seas added to the water space every minute. Soon the Denes were converted into a surging lake, which enlarged rapidly. It spread to the foot of Christchurch score and washed through the streets. Fortunately the wind dropped before any more disaster. Looking from Mariners score the district below appeared as one extensive water area with houses dotted here and there and posts sticking up grotesquely. The water splashed like a miniature sea. They are mainly poor humble folk. Mrs. Hales perched on the roof of a cottage and stayed until a boat came and a beach man brought her down. Some men sacrificed half a day. It was an example of how poor people help each other in times of emergency and danger. Some of the houses are mere hovels. The sea wall erected some time ago stood the strain, and without it there would have been more damage. The beach people are great at tidying up; some poor women were in tears as they surveyed their muddy interior of rooms, generally so spick and span. In clogs and top boots men and women worked with a will to get the water out. It will be weeks before the houses are dry. The new gasometer was surrounded with water, and the model yacht pond was blotted out.*

A Relief Fund was set up by Reverend David Dickson, Mayor E. Tuttle gave coal and Francis Lucas MP gave £10 to his constituents to help their suffering.

New dock works which were being excavated for the Great Eastern Railway became a scene of desolation and destruction. The floods covered machinery and toppled cranes. Trenches that took weeks to excavate were filled with shingle and sand and had to be pumped empty.

As well as bringing in much income from fish, the maritime trade provided significant employment on land. Many boats were built or repaired in the Inner Harbour. The Swing Bridge allowed them passage out to sea. The boat sailing through is LT 956 *George Borrow*, built 1902 and sunk by U-boat 11th August 1915. The buildings on the right, on the north bank of Lake Lothing, include the Custom House. Behind the boat are the "iron works", built in the 1850s by the North of Europe Steam Navigation Company, who conducted Peto's cattle trade with Denmark. In the distance, the crane is a sheerleg, used to install engines and boilers into boats.

With the vast increase in the fishing industry that took place in the second half of the 19th century, it gave opportunity for related employment to spring up to supply the shipping needs. One such shop was the Co-operative Ship Stores Ltd. in Suffolk Road who advertised themselves as stores of high quality, and sold nets, ropes, corks, oils, carbide and were general ship chandlers. The East Anglian Ice and Cold Storage Company were makers of clear table ice, and their output was 250 tons of ice a day. There was the Gourock Rope Works in Battery Green Road. R J Latten Ltd., timber merchants, made fish boxes as well as other boxes, fencing and prime coffin boards.

From about 1880, the Inner Harbour, as well as containing some commercial quays, became a focus for many essential support industries related to boat building. This is a view of Lake Lothing taken from the bridge. Along with the slipways and dry docks, there were several timber yards, iron works and engineering works. An oil mill and gasometer also appear on the maps of 1890 and 1904.

A sheerleg on the north quay hoisting a boiler into a steam drifter, built by John Chambers.

Such was Lowestoft's success that many boat builders came from elsewhere in the UK. Henry Reynolds for example was born in Beccles in 1834, and John Chambers was born at Gorleston in 1841. The latter formed a partnership with the local family of Colbys which was known as Colby and Chambers. Both Reynolds and Chambers lived close to their shipyards on the northern banks of Lake Lothing, in Denmark Road.

Samuel Richards, who was born in Cornwall in 1853, was the son of a boat builder. In 1875 he set sail to Lowestoft possessing only 25 golden sovereigns, and established his own shipbuilding business on the south side of Kirkley Ham, where there was a natural slope to the water, an ideal position, known as Sam's Wharf. After a few years the shipyard moved to the site adjoining Lucas Brothers joinery works, which became C&E Morton Ltd. In the 1880s the yard built about 100 sailing drifters that cost £360 each and later built steam-propelled vessels.

Left: Along the Inner Harbour were Jewson, Lacey & Lincoln, W T Jeckells the sail maker and Craske Ltd. Their boat *Craske* is moored alongside. In the fore of this picture is a sunken steam drifter, with only its funnel and masts above water level. The crowd on the left have congregated to look at it. Craske Ltd. of Bridge Chambers were coal and coke merchants. They advertised as importers of best quality sea-borne and rail-borne coal, with branches at Lerwick, Newlyn, Penzance and Plymouth. Steamers could be supplied with coal by them at short notice by day or night and during the First World War they were on the Admiralty list.

As the area around the Inner Harbour was largely devoted to industry, much of it involving wood storage, there was a great risk of fire. There were fires at the oil cake mill, net factory, box factory and timber yards, as well as at shops and houses. Fires could be particularly devastating because of the time the volunteer fire brigade took to respond, as each member had a day job and no telephone. Mr. T E Thirtle, who was captain of the brigade, ran the ironmongers shop near the town hall and was a keen amateur dramatist. Once he had grown a beard for the part and was in the process of cutting it off when the fire alarm went, so he attended the fire wearing half a beard. In 1911, another poor fireman came a cropper whilst returning from the blaze at the Co-op at Oulton Broad, riding home on his motorbike. He had just reached the cemetery when his tyre burst, he was flung off his bike, and fell on his head with his helmet jammed over his nose.

Around 1900 a horse-drawn fire engine was introduced which carried a steam pump, which was kept in the fire station in St. Peter's Street. However, the horses, which were not kept with the engine, were used for other purposes and had to be caught and harnessed before the engine could go. In early September 1907, a week before the R.J. Latten fire, a fire broke out at 56 Lorne Road, Kirkley where Mr. and Mrs. George Warman lived. Mrs. Warman had gone out for a walk, leaving her kettle on the oil stove ready for tea, it being 3.30 p.m. on a Sunday afternoon. Unfortunately the stove burst into flames and the fire soon spread to her linen, and the rest of her kitchen. Firemen Hood, Lamb and others quickly arrived, and very soon the fire was quenched, with the help of the neighbours forming a chain, by using water pails and passing them along to each other. Captain Thirtle and the police were present, but no fire engine, which arrived an hour later, at 4.30 p.m., after the fire had been put out, due to a difficulty in procuring horses.

On the morning of 19th September 1907, R. J. Latten Ltd. of Commercial Road, caught fire. Robert Latten was born at Norwich in 1860 and moved to Lowestoft, where he lived at 280 London Road. His company bought English and foreign hardwood and made all kinds of boxes including fish boxes, seed trays, fruit trays, apple boxes and mineral water boxes. They also sent cut bundles of boxwood to any part of the United Kingdom and locally known as the Box Factory. Large stocks of English timber were always available, including prime coffin boards and all kinds of fencing materials. In the First World War they were contractors to the War Office for packing cases.

This fire caused thousands of pounds worth of damage. Workshops were gutted, machinery destroyed and boxes and stacks of wood were consumed, leaving only charred remains. The fire, which was believed to have started when some shavings ignited, raged until the evening. It was, however, excellent entertainment for the whole family.

Joey, who took this picture from his bedroom window, and posted it to a friend, said that it was blazing for thirteen hours, and that people all thought that their row of houses would catch alight. The fire brigade can just be made out in the centre of this shot, directing their jets towards the factory. With so much wood about, fires were almost inevitable.

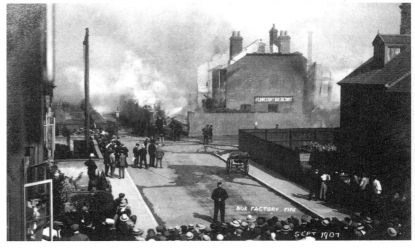

Jewsons' extensive Timber Yard was on the South Quay. On 30th May 1911, the piles of planed wood and large stacks of fish boxes were dry from long storage, and the hot May sunshine. As police constable Goodwin went by, he saw smoke and flames coming from them and he raised the alarm at 9.15 p.m. In less than five minutes the whole of the stacks were blazing furiously. The Great Eastern Railway tug *Despatch*, under the charge of Captain Sterry, was moored close by, and this gave assistance by pumping water over the fire. Additionally Jewsons' own fire brigade, from Belvedere Road premises, used their appliance. It was not until 10 p.m. that the fire engine, with Captain Thirtle crossed over the bridge, and ten minutes later they began to apply their powerful jets. Dense cloud and flying brands and sparks choked the firemen, who kept on working to midnight. Messrs Lacy and Lincoln, next door, had a few broken tiles. The fire had to be watched, as it kept breaking out again in the night, and into the next day, after the fire engine had left.

When the old oil cake mills in Commercial Road caught fire on 22nd May 1904, H.M.S. *Hearty* and a tug came to help put out the fire.

On 25th March, 1911, a fire broke out at Leaches' shop, at the corner of London Road and Suffolk Road. The ground floor sold oil, paint, varnish, wallpaper and the yard had tanks of paraffin. A policeman blew his whistle when the fire was spotted, but by the time the fire was put out, the store was destroyed.

With the phenomenal growth in the fishing industry, Lowestoft enjoyed a time as a premier port and holiday resort, and greatly expanded. Many people had moved to Lowestoft to set up business or to work, even before Mr. Spashett's advertisement. Mr. Spashett, President of the Lowestoft and District Incorporated Chamber of Commerce, wrote enticingly in the 1928 Town guide, to manufacturers: *Lowestoft enjoys facilities for transport of merchandise by rail and water, numerous buildings and sites with waterside frontage and railways adjoining, are obtainable for factory purposes. There is adequate local labour, convenient services of trams and motor-buses, and knowledge that work people are well housed under the best sanitary conditions, and are living in what is probably the most healthy resort in the country. Engineering businesses and factories in the manufacture of motor bodies and electrical fittings have recently been opened in the town.*

The land along London Road North became increasingly valuable for retail purposes, where once several affluent residents had lived in villas with large gardens. One such person was a medical practitioner and surgeon from Northumberland, Dr. Wilson Tyson, who lived at 109 London Road North. His little daughter Evelyn, who was born in 1900, is seen here in a pony and trap in their front garden. The previous owner had been Dr. Francis Samuel Worthington who lived there for over 30 years, and had been born in Lowestoft as the son of a doctor. He employed several staff including a nurse, Sarah A. Bacon, who resided there throughout his residence. This house was eventually demolished and Woolworth's was built in its place.

Looking north from the post office (on the left), are some large trees, which remind us of the more rural past of London Road North. Behind them we can make out a large house, and in front stands the villa's garden wall. This house was later demolished to make way for shops. On the right here once stood The Grove, a house with an estate of more than six acres, from Waveney Road up to the Marina, and extending eastwards to Whapload Road. Mrs. Mary Roddam was a physician's widow who moved from Ipswich to Lowestoft in the 1850s and lived in this house. She described herself as a proprietor of houses and a fundholder. When she died in 1884, at the age of 94, the estate (except for the most eastern section, which she

left to her neighbour Dr. Clubbe, together with the fence) was bought by the proprietor of the Suffolk Hotel and was soon covered with buildings such as Tuttles, as well as those which can be seen here on the right. Several of these houses and shops were designed by architect William Chambers, who also was the architect for the Jubilee Bridge over the Ravine. However, no pubs were allowed to be built since the purchaser also owned the Harbour Inn, and did not want his trade affected. This scene is photographed from just before the junction of Surrey Street and Beach Road. Immediately on the right are Cross & Co., china dealers, at 56 London Road, next door to W. Howlett & Son the music dealers. Jarrold & Sons Ltd, stationers, publishers and bookseller, are on the corner of Beach Road (and remained there until recent years).

This is the optician shop of Charles J. Evans at 99 London Road North, situated next to the old British Home Stores. Evans advertised on the front cover of the 1924 Kelly's Directory as having the *Highest qualifications for sight testing*. He also had another shop in Southwold.

With the arrival of the railway and the growth of trade, tourism and industry, Lowestoft was expanding, south into Kirkley and north towards Gunton, as well as inland along the banks of Lake Lothing. All these people needed to get to work. Until the middle of the nineteenth century, travel in the Lowestoft area was fairly limited. Farmers brought animals to market along drove roads, traders used packways to transport goods for sale, fishermen went down to the beach to get to their boats, villagers came to the town markets and shops to buy. Most people walked. For longer journeys you could take the mail coach, ride with a carrier, or take a horse or horse-drawn wagonette (pictured here). The bells on the harness gave them the nickname of "Jingles".

Above: The main hub for onward transportation to and from the railway station was the Royal Plain where the Harbour Hotel (just left of centre) and Royal Hotel were situated. From here, tourists were taken for day trips, and local public transport picked up passengers.

Right: John J W Reeve, who was one of Lowestoft's first motor car taxi drivers, is posing, waiting for passengers on the Royal Plain outside the Yacht Club. His family business previously owned horse-drawn carriages which operated from The Stables, in Mill Road.

Below: The Royal Plain remained a transport hub throughout the 20th Century, with the main office of Belles coaches nearby and the coach pick-up stop for local excursions, on Royal Plain itself.

In 1882 plans were made to construct a horse-drawn tramway in Lowestoft, but this did not materialise, nor did an 1898 proposal to construct an electric tramway from Yarmouth to Kessingland. After the arrival of electricity in Lowestoft, in 1901, the Corporation of Lowestoft used powers given in the Light Railways Act 1896 to lay tram lines from Belle Vue Park to Pakefield, with a depot in Rotterdam Road. They aimed to lease the tram lines to the East Anglian Light Railway Co. for 28 years. Eventually the company withdrew because the Lowestoft Corporation was not prepared to pay enough, and so the Lowestoft Corporation constructed, and ran, the tramway themselves. Throughout its life the tramway was run on a very tight budget. From the outset the contractors selected to build the lines and sheds, provide the uniforms and ticket paraphernalia and everything else necessary, were those who gave the cheapest estimates.

LOWESTOFT SWING BRIDGE

G. A. Bruce drew up plans for running electric tram cables under the harbour, using steel pipes supplied by Babcock & Wilcox. Running electric cables underneath the water permitted the bridge to be swung open without undue interference with the overhead cables. This swing bridge replaced the original one in 1897, and was one of several new additions to Lowestoft to commemorate Queen Victoria's Jubilee. Some others were the clock in the tower of St. John's Church, and the Ravine Bridge. The swing bridge lasted until 1969, and was replaced by a raising bridge in 1972. However, many locals continue to describe the bridge, when delayed by its opening, as being "off" rather than "up".

Parliament required the Board of Trade to make regulations to protect the public from danger, as could be expected given that the trams were a novel and potentially lethal intrusion to a highway still used by horse-drawn vehicles (as seen below next to the harbour master's house). Safety regulations were drawn up about the use of electrical power on the overhead trolley system, the tram braking system, warning bells and whistles, fog lights and front and rear oil lamps. The speed at which trams travelled must have been a particular nightmare for the driver, being specifically prescribed at 4, 6, 8, 10 and 12 m.p.h. For example between Denmark Road and Rotterdam Road trams could go 12 m.p.h., but only 6 m.p.h. between Denmark Road and London Road, and only 4 m.p.h. on the curves between Denmark Road and London Road. A tram consisted of tons of metal that screeched and clattered along over points with sparks flying. To bring it to an emergency halt, the driver would apply the hand brake and throw a bucket of sand onto the line.

To accommodate the tram line, road widening was necessary in places, and this extended from Old Market Street to Blue Anchor Plain. It also necessitated demolishing the buildings seen in this picture, which was taken around 1880.

Benjamin Saunders the butcher, as owner occupier of 133 High Street, received £1,600 compensation, whilst Fred Morse, who owned both 130 High Street and the Globe Inn, was offered £1,500, but after his appeal he eventually got £1,800. Arthur Dann, who occupied the Globe Inn, and Thomas J. Martin the occupier of 130 High Street, were each offered £80, but their appeals secured £90.

Frontages were reduced in some parts of the High Street, and in London Road South, between Windsor and Lorne Park Roads. Some of those who lost their buildings in London Road South included Fred Mummery, at number 85, who received £950, and next door neighbour Nathan Corbyn who was offered £1,000. Fred Morse was offered £1,800, for 78 London Road South, which included the Royal Oak pub, and Messrs. Sterry of 205 and 207 London Road South were offered £3,000.

Plenty of work was generated for local inhabitants, and many arrangements made during the two year period before the tramway was opened. Fifteen tram cars were ordered, with a further four the following year. The tram lines, which were made in Antwerp, eventually arrived by ship, after a lot of nail biting, the day before the scheduled ceremonial line-laying at Pakefield. Uniforms, buttons, tickets and punches were purchased, tram stops and shelters installed, fare prices decided and insurance for workers taken out.

The trams consisted of a fleet of eleven open-top double deckers which seated 48 people, and four single decker trams that seated 38. The following year four more trams were added, making a total of nineteen trams. They all had wooden seats.

Above: The opening ceremony of the first tram took place on 22nd July 1903. All the London newspapers and technical magazines were invited to the ceremony, and to lunch. Also accommodation at the Empire Hotel for two nights was provided. A procession of five trams decorated with flags and bunting, travelled the length of the tram line. Here it has just crossed the bridge heading south past the horse-drawn cabs waiting for passengers by the Royal Plain. The first tram (seen in the picture above) was driven a mile by the Mayor, Mr. Lancelot Orde, bearing a photograph of the King , and carried the Mayors and Mayoresses of Norwich, Great Yarmouth and Beccles. The second tram carried a picture of the Queen and was filled with aldermen, councillors and borough officials of Lowestoft and their families. The third tram carried contractors and engineers and was a single deck car. The fourth was occupied by the press and the last carried other invited guests.

There were two tram shelters, one, seen here, at Pier Terrace, and the other at the North Parade terminus. They were painted dark green at the base, green and white at the top and had white window frames. Pier Terrace, which was built as a commercial row, is on the right where H. Jenkins had his photographic store, and where Waller & Son sold sweets and home-made jelly. The tram is heading for Belle Vue Park. Although they were much appreciated by the public, when Pakefield requested a shelter for their terminus, sufficient money was never found for it.

The tram drivers, too, had to brave the elements, with both ends of the tram open. Lowestoft, being the most easterly town in Britain, receives the full force of the biting wind as it sweeps in across the sea. In winter drivers faced all weathers. They wore boots and dressed in thick clothes and oilskins to keep out the worst, as there was no glass window in front of them. It was not unknown for them to end their shift with icicles dangling from their whiskers.

Discipline also was strict. Uniforms had to be smart, and buttons polished daily. Leaving a passenger behind, or who was still approaching the tram stop, could incur a punishment of two or three days suspension. Entering a pub in uniform or rudeness to a passenger resulted in one day suspension, and repeatedly failing to collect fares led to dismissal. To cap all this, the wages for drivers and conductors in Lowestoft were much lower than elsewhere (the Corporation paid out only £3,500 or so in wages in 1905).

One driver, apparently, allowed an Italian circus master on board with his performing bear. On ascending the upper deck, the bear paraded up and down to the playing of the accordion. The passengers, however, hurriedly descended the steps at both ends! In 1909 the principal attraction at the Hippodrome was W. Permane and his live teddy bears. He was the *possessor of the only talking bear in the world*. We don't know what that bear said to the driver, but after then no animals were allowed on board that were bigger than a lap dog.

Trams in Lowestoft were such a new event, that other towns with more experience of trams (Ilford, Yarmouth, Ramsgate, Dover, Bournemouth & Norwich) were often asked for advice for example, concerning how they charged their fares, particularly with regard to children. Despite learning that towns such as Ilford charged half fare for travelling to and from school, Lowestoft decided not to adopt this, until the Chairman of the Education committee made a request.

Originally, tram fares cost a penny from Pakefield to the railway station. On the occasion of Buffalo Bill's Wild West performance at Pakefield, however, the Tramway Committee decided to double the fare, in order to get more revenue, but later they changed their minds. This was just as well because the local newspaper inserted Buffalo Bill's advert on the same day as the Tramway Manager reported that they had been making very good money. The latter read: *Another good week, the Lowestoft tramcars continue to be well patronized. During the week ending Tuesday night, the cars carried 74,138 passengers, the money taken totalling £385 10s. 6d. Regatta day is included, £71 being taken. Since the opening day 470,997 passengers have been carried and the total receipts in the 6 weeks are £2,294 13s. 10d. We should imagine that this is a record for any town the size and population of Lowestoft.* Indeed in 1905, the General Manager noted that over £10,000 was taken that year, mostly in coppers.

Perhaps in order to create goodwill, and to generate custom, the Corporation had the trams decorated on special occasions, with paper flowers or lights and sometimes staff even dressed up. This was one of the four single deck cars owned by the Lowestoft Corporation Tramways, which were considered to be luxurious. This tram is decorated with flags and flowers, probably for the carnival of 1924. There is a notice stating *Fare 6d. anywhere*, while the driver poses on the left and the conductor on the right.

When the First World War broke out, visitors left the town and the fares dropped drastically. In addition trams stopped early. The last tram to leave Suffolk Corner for both ends of the town, had been at 9.15 p.m.. It was decided, however, that for public safety the cars were to leave the terminus at 7 p.m. and be off the road by 7.45 p.m. This upset some people who felt it to be too early, especially since the trams in Great Yarmouth still ran until after 11 p.m.

Aside from damage to the car sheds and lines caused by Zeppelin raids, the other main impact on the tramways was the employment of women to fill posts left by men called up. In 1916 Herbert Saunders, the General Manager of the Lowestoft Corporation Tramways, wrote to the Board of Trade stating that he wanted to train women conductors to act as drivers on the electric tramways, and wondered if any objection would be raised. He added that the system consisted practically of one route three miles long with no dangerous gradient or curves and was given authorization. The local newspaper took up the story, saying that they were not surprised at the decision as there were already women conductors on the trams: *They carry out their not too pleasant duties remarkably well. They are cheerful, courteous and obliging. They do not whistle and sing. They are not looking out on the ships at sea when they should be engaged in keeping their eyes on would be passengers. They do not want to discuss the weather and crops with all and sundry, and if they see an old lady, or one of the other sex, who needs a hand, they readily give a helping lift on to the car. These kindnesses are little perhaps in themselves but they count for much and they certainly help the earning capacity of the trams. So all round they have done well, and therefore if women conductors have proved so adaptable and are so entirely successful, why not women drivers.*

One of the women recruits was Olive Charlish. LCT stands for Lowestoft Corporation Tramways. Her son Frank Wernham relates the story of his parents meeting and marrying. He said: *My father Leonard Wernham had been a regular soldier since 1907, and was in the trenches from 1914. In July 1917 he was in the second battle of Ypres and was wounded for the second time, having also been once gassed. This wound was serious enough for him to be returned to the UK and hospitalized for almost twelve months, at the end of which he was sent to convalesce in a home, which had been a girl's school, in Lowestoft. As his condition improved he got in the habit of travelling by tram down to the sea front in order to sit on the beach (as an invalid soldier he would have enjoyed free travel). His injured leg was still stiff so he was obliged to sit at the front of the tram behind the driver, which often was my mother. They chatted, I believe that he used to take sandwiches for her, at all events romance blossomed, and in 1919 they were married at Kirkley Church. My father was still in the army, but with a desk job, as a Quarter Master Sergeant, and he was sent to London to work as part of the demobilisation programme, taking my mother with him.*

When Olive resigned, before her marriage, she received a letter from her employer stating: *I would like to take this opportunity of saying that during the time you have been on the cars you have given me every satisfaction in the way you have discharged your duties. Your general conduct has been most praiseworthy. As I understand you are getting married shortly, I take this opportunity of wishing you every happiness and prosperity in your married life.*

At the end of the war the active service employees of the Lowestoft Corporation Electricity and Tramway Dept. were given a Welcome Home dinner at the Royal Hotel. The menu had a touch of humour, referring to the food in tramway terms, such as electric clear soup, and axle grease sauce. Entertainment was given by the women who had carried on while the men were on Active Service. Those present included the Mayor and Mayoress, Deputy Mayor and council. There were songs, recitations and the appearance of Tom Wheatley who was ventriloquist at the Lowestoft Hippodrome. Everyone enjoyed themselves. However, naturally the men wanted their jobs back, so the employment of women tram drivers came to an end.

The trams were very successful, with over two million passengers a year up to 1909. The organised public transport network increased, with petrol buses being introduced in 1927, as tramway feeders. However these were the downfall of the trams. They were cheaper to run, and as the original 28 year lease period came to an end, it was decided to replace the trams with buses completely.

After 28 years service the last tram ran on 8th May 1931. It returned to the shed in Denmark Road wearing a wreath of laurel and lilies and was driven by Mr. N Rudd, who had driven the trams for the entire 28 years. The tram fleet had clocked up eight million miles between them, and there had never been a fatal accident. One of the trams has been preserved and can be seen at the East Anglia Transport Museum at Carlton Colville.

Along with improved transport links, the growth of Lowestoft demanded leisure facilities for the populace. Lowestoft did not have any parks until the 1870s when the Lowestoft Improvement Committee decided to turn the old common at North Battery Green into a park. This was Belle Vue Park and was opened to the public in 1874.

On 29th August 1887 the Ravine Bridge, linking North Parade with Belle Vue, was opened to mark Queen Victoria's Golden Jubilee. It was described as a beautiful, elegant cast iron design, with decorative balustrade and timber decking. Designed by architect William Oldham Chambers, of Chambers & Roberts, its span was 70 feet, and 30 feet above the Ravine. The first mayor of Lowestoft, William Youngman, paid for the bridge, and the opening by the M.P. Sir Savile Crossley marked the second anniversary of the granting of a Charter of Incorporation to the new Borough of Lowestoft. The idea of a footbridge had first come up in 1856, in the patriotic aftermath of the Crimea War, when a committee was set up to carry the idea through and subscriptions were invited. But when the secretary moved away, the whole thing fell through.

Ten years later, in 1897, the town corporation bought Sparrow's Nest Gardens as a pleasure park. This had once belonged to Robert Sparrow, who was a wealthy man, from Worlingham. Sparrow's Nest was his summer residence.

The area to the north of the town was developed more for the locals than the tourists (who were mainly around the South Beach). In particular many other leisure facilities were established on the Gunton Denes, at the foot of the Ravine (seen below), where there were also allotments.

MODEL YACHT POND, LOWESTOFT.

Above: In 1889 the model yacht pond was opened on Gunton Denes by the mayor. Races were held in the summer, and yachts could be stored in a shed. After the First World War the pond was closed and filled in. In the distance on the left of the picture are a row of beach huts, while on the right a smack sails past.

Below: In 1926 new gardens were created on the site where the model yacht pond had formerly been. On the left is the edge of the cricket oval with the pavilion, and on the right the tennis courts. Behind the tennis is the miniature golf course, then a paddling pool and finally the swimming pool. In the foreground a sign threatens prosecution for any one throwing rubbish down the cliff slope.

The Jubilee of King George V was in May 1935, and many Lowestoft celebrations took place in the cricket ground on the Denes in July. Here school children have made a Union Jack Flag formation. Iris Porter was here and has vivid memories: *I remember that we were in groups of different colours, red, white and blue, and that we marched around and practised a lot.* In 1885 Lowestoft became a borough, and 1935 was also its 50th year and jubilee, so the two celebrations were combined.

Amongst other communal pastimes, in which men could display their strength and prowess, was tug of war. Here some of the Hook and Durrant families are sporting their trophies in a photograph taken around 1900. Both were fishing families.

Oulton Broad also became a focus of pleasure Sailing, being very close to Lowestoft, as well as retaining some industrial functions. Yacht racing is a well-established event at Oulton Broad, and Regatta Week was always popular.

The boat *Elsinore*, is the pleasure craft in the foreground. In the background are some wherries loading malt or delivering grain to the Swonnell & Son Maltings building. The maltings were built between 1900 and 1902, when Swonnells moved from Nine Elms to Oulton Broad in order to be in the heart of the barley country. They quickly built up a reputation for fine malts, and were one of the few in the country to produce both pale and coloured malts. They expanded in the 1920s with the addition of two more maltings, improved apparatus for roasting malt and grain and hydrocarbon burners. They worked from September to May and in summer cleaned the machinery. Three cats were kept to kill the mice. The business closed in 1968 and the building is now apartments.

This motor boat named *Brooke 2*, seen on Oulton Broad, was fitted with an engine built by Brooke Marine. John Walter Brooke was born in 1840 at Barnsley. He came to Lowestoft in 1873 and bought the iron foundry of Cushion & Langly in Clapham Road in 1874 (which was later extended to the Adrian Works at 47 Alexandra Road). He manufactured steam capstans for fishing boats, double action pumps and lift and hoist machinery for marine use. In 1887 he fitted a steam engine into his new river launch Nellie, which was built by Richards, and from this time began to specialise in engines. As well as being a successful business man, he

was on the council from 1887 and served as a county magistrate until 1902, being elected mayor three years in succession from 1913 to 1915. Brooke Marine was based on the north shore of Lake Lothing, where they built car and boat engines, as well as engines for some of the first aeroplanes. The first Brooke car went on the road in 1902. In conjunction with Reynolds, who built the boats, Brooke Marine constructed 40 motor boats between 1904 and 1907. These were very good, reliable engines that achieved world acclaim, particularly in motor boat racing, when between 1906 and 1918 Brooke racing launches won races all over the world from Cowes to Monaco. Many of their boats competed in the inshore Motor Boat races on Oulton Broad, beside Everitts Park which took place on Whit Mondays.

Whit Monday motor boat racing began in 1904 at Oulton Broad with the formation of the British Motor Boat Club, although it only took off in 1905. In this year *Brooke's Baby 1*, owned by Mawdesley Brooke, took first prize. These Whit Monday races became a national event and people flocked to see them. They were also good for Brooke's business, and J.W. Brooke sponsored a silver rose bowl prize, the *Brooke Trophy*, for oil motor boats.

The photograph above is taken from the north side of Oulton Broad. Until 1929, Everitts Park was a private field known as Mr. Everitt's Meadow so members of the public could not view the races from there. A friend of Mawdesley Brooke was Howard Hollingsworth, a businessman who was chairman of an Oxford Street shop, owner of the London Road department store and a racing enthusiast, who entered racing boats at Monaco and Burnham-on-Crouch. It was he who bought the park on Mr. Everitt's death and gave it to the town to commemorate Nicholas Everitt who was an author, lawyer and naturalist.

The area along the South Beach continued to develop as a place where the sea could be enjoyed by tourists and locals alike, and events were held in its public spaces. The Proclamation of King George and Queen Mary at the Royal Plain, Lowestoft May 1910. On the right are a detachment of soldiers, while there are naval personnel and scouts just in front of the column. Between them, the mayor and other local dignitaries read the Proclamation.

LOWESTOFT. THE YACHT BASIN AND HARBOUR. (94)

This is an overview of the harbour, taken after 1903 when the trams were introduced. The new pavilion and Promenade Pier has been erected, and the yacht club gardens have been laid out. The Inner South Pier, stretching out into the centre of the picture, is where two tug paddle steamers are moored. The small pavilion in front of it advertises pleasure boats for hire, while various elegantly dressed people pass in the foreground. However, in the midst of the leisure and fun there was hardship: by the fence are two elderly gents earning a living from passers by. One is selling small items, the other, who has a wooden leg, appears to be cleaning shoes.

Adverts for holiday accommodation frequently mentioned their close proximity to the South Pier, which was part of the harbour wall, and many postcards carried messages from people who had enjoyed strolling along it. Just in front of the trio in the centre of this picture is a photographer taking a snap. This was usually in the hope of selling a copy to the tourists photographed. This scene probably shows Regatta Day, when all the flags were flown.

The photo below is taken from the pavilion. On Regatta Day there were boat races and other water sports. The South Pier was a focal point with swimming and aquatic sports taking place in the harbour, next to the pavilion. There was also a fete on the pier, with a firework display closing the events.

The pavilion, where teas and refreshments could be bought, was built around 1890. Beside it can be seen the bandstand, which is in use. It replaced the reading room, which had been erected by Peto, but which burnt down in July 1885. The *Illustrated London News* gave this account: *Burning of Lowestoft Promenade Pier. The fire which broke out on the 29th in the floor of the reading room erected on the promenade pier at Lowestoft, entirely destroyed the centre part of the pier with the handsome structures upon it, the reading room, the pagoda for the band of music, and a small kiosk used as a bazaar. It was soon after 11 o'clock at night that the fire was discovered, and the efforts to quench it were of no avail till next morning. We are indebted to a local correspondent for a sketch of the scene upon this disastrous occasion. The damage is estimated at £20,000. The pier is the property of the Great Eastern Railway Company. The South Pier will be speedily put into a state for the accommodation of visitors to Lowestoft during the season.*

During the holiday season a band played everyday in the bandstand on the South Pier.

Above: Soon after 1905, races took place on the sea off the South Pier with both yachts and motor boats (here seen with a smack). Mawdsley Brooke won many trophies. In 1929 The Daily Mirror sponsored the Daily Mirror International Challenge Trophy for B Class outboard motors and various eliminating rounds were held in various parts of the country. The final took place off Lowestoft on 13th September. It was a twelve lap course, starting at the South Pier, going past Claremont Pier to Pakefield, then to a buoy out at sea and back to South Pier. There were 22 starters but the race was won by J Drummonds of Glasgow in *Gang Warily*.

Below: The piers were popular venues for sea angling, for which there were competitions. During autumn and winter vast shoals of whiting approached the coast, followed later by cod and codling. Both men and ladies enjoyed the sport of fishing from the piers, beach and little boats. Some of the best catches could be had at night.

On 29th October 1910 the Lowestoft Sea Angling Society had a club match on the South Pier. It was the qualifying round for the Brooke Cup (again made available by J.W. Brooke). Between 2.30 p.m. and 5.30 p.m. a total of 157 lbs. of fish were caught; the largest cod was 29.5 lbs. The photo shows the prize catches, posing in front of the Yacht Club.

This was just one match during the season. There was also a hospital match which was open to all comers, and the Ladies Sea Angling Society competed for a silver cup at the Claremont Pier. Seventeen fished, but sport was not good as the weather was windy and very cold, but the ladies stood it well till the finish. At the 3rd round the prizes were taken by

1st Mrs Hildyard 3lbs. 13 oz.

2nd Mrs Cook 2lbs. 5 oz.

3rd Miss Rose 2lbs. 3 oz.

Ladies were invited to join the club by applying to Mrs Hildyard of Hevingham House, London Road South.

Angling was not restricted to competitions. Boys fished in the harbour, which was open to the public. Codling fishing went on until the end of April when dab fishing commenced. The bait consisted of small rag worms, or pieces of lug worm, or tiny cubes of fresh herring.

At the beginning of the 20th century Lowestoft was prospering. Industry had expanded, the fishing trade boomed and the holiday trade was well-established. Large house parties took over boarding house accommodation. The Esplanade Hotel, was the last of the Morton Peto grand houses on the esplanade. It was a 40 bedroom hotel, and when sold in the 1930s had an electric lift and a large car park. The proprietors from about 1913 were Mr. and Mrs. T Jenner. Mr. Jenner was on the general purposes committee of the Lowestoft Chamber of Commerce, and his hotel was advertised in their book as a high class and unlicensed hotel, situated in the centre of the promenade, overlooking the sea. It was especially recommended for comfort and cuisine, with well-appointed public rooms, dance rooms, and large and comfortable bedrooms.

South View and Wellesley House, was a first class boarding house in Wellington Esplanade. Proprietors of this establishment in 1902 were Mrs. Westgate senior & daughter Mrs. Jenner. It was centrally situated, close to the pier, and with excellent sea views. There were fifty beds and a reception room, all with electric light. It advertised that it was a quarter of a minute from the shore, had excellent cuisine, the tariff was moderate, and there were special winter terms. When old Mrs. Westgate died her daughter and son-in-law Mr. Jenner, became proprietors.This picture was taken during the holiday season in 1906, depicting many of the guests staying then. The correspondent, from London, wrote on the postcard: *We like Lowestoft immensely, it's lively and bracing, weather glorious and bathing good.*

Left: Tourists did not just come to Lowestoft by train. From 1897, a paddle steamer service ran from London to Great Yarmouth and was very popular. Originally the steamers went to the harbour. However, with the growth of South Lowestoft along the Kirkley Cliffs (with the many hotels there), it was thought sensible to build the Claremont Pier, opened in 1903, to serve this area. It was built by the Coast Development Company for Belle Steamers, as a landing stage for boats from London and Great Yarmouth, and had a T-piece to enable boats to stop there. At Royal Plain, there was a taxi rank of horse-drawn gigs nearby to take people the next stage of their journey.

A day trip from Lowestoft to Clacton cost seven shillings and sixpence for cabin class, and a return trip to London was twelve shillings and sixpence before the Second World War. This all ended with the war and the last paddle steamer to call at Lowestoft carried 3,500 London evacuee school children.

Below: Just along the cliff from the Claremont Pier was this thatched house next to a putting green.

CLAREMONT PIER.
LOWESTOFT.

Tourism brought different opportunities to Lowestoft residents. The Barnard family kept Shetland ponies at Barnard's Farm in Laundry Lane, now Eastern Way, which they used to give pony and trap rides from the Royal Plain down the Middle Drive to the Claremont Pier. Up on the North Denes Beach they gave donkey rides, near the swimming pool, until the Second World War. Mr. Jones was a little man with waxed moustache who habitually wore a cap. He gave children rides in a donkey cart, and on ponies, in Wellington Gardens from before the Second World War until he died in the 1950s.

Right: Mons Boys' sea pleasure trips were a typical leisure pastime for holidaymakers. The boats were frequently manned by retired fishermen and did trips round the harbour and to view larger vessels anchored out at sea.

Right: The *Elizabeth Simpson* lifeboat was described in her log book as the fastest and finest boat on the east coast. It was presented to Gorleston in 1889 and during her 50 years service was launched 119 times. She had a crew of 21 and was capable of carrying 150 passengers. The boat was 47 feet long with foresail and mizzen sail, and had seven pairs of oars. After the Second World War she became a privately owned pleasure craft and gave pleasure trips around Lowestoft and Oulton Broad.

Above: On the South Beach was the little concert hall (known as the South Beach Pavilion) owned by Will Edwards, the popular London comedian. It was wrecked by high tides caused by a storm on September 11th 1912 in a sad culmination to a successful season. The Lowestoft Standard reported on 2nd August 1912 that: *Splendid business still continues at Mr Will Edwards' popular resort, which is not surprising in view of the excellent and varied programme presented.* Shows were twice daily at 3.30 p.m. & 9 p.m., costing threepence for the afternoon and sixpence or a shilling in the evening.

Left: Ricardo Sacco was a hunger artist act in the circus and fairs. He would sit in a booth and the crowds would peer at him. He held the World's Fasting Record of 52 days and eight hours. He was in Lowestoft in November 1909 when this photograph was autographed.

Below: The summer season of 1912 saw this group performing at the Claremont Pier: back row from left to right: Mr. Ernest Penfold, Mr. Vere Denys, Mr. Herbert E Williams, and front row left to right Mr. Charles Resti, Miss Ethel Netherway and Miss Agnes Orrell.

World War One brought an abrupt halt to the relaxed atmosphere of former years. Visitors left the town, and even the trams noticed the drastic drop in income. Before the war, submarines and naval ships had visited Lowestoft. Then alterations were made to the harbour to enable larger ships to come and go. This led to rumours that Lowestoft was to be a major naval base, as indeed came to pass. Lowestoft played an important part in the war, with both the harbour facilities and the wealth of maritime expertise of the fishermen being called upon.

A flotilla of submarines was at Lowestoft Harbour on 2nd March 1910. These C class numbers 1 to 9 arrived from Harwich and were berthed in the yacht basin, where the crews can be seen working on them, while a group of fishermen look on. They were accompanied by their parent ship named *Thames* and a torpedo boat, which anchored in the Roads off Lowestoft.

Some of the submarines left the harbour next day, watched by a crowd of men on the dock, and went for manoeuvres, the torpedo boat accompanying. It was low water when the craft left and one of them grounded on the Newcome Sands. The parent ship was standing by and the Pakefield lifeboat went out in response to what were said to be signals of distress. After a short time the submarine floated again. The majority of the submarines returned in the afternoon and were, this time, berthed in the Inner Harbour, only C1 remaining in the yacht basin.

The harbour, with its useful rail connections, was used during the war to store all sorts of military equipment. Here oil has been brought in tankers by rail to the dock side, on the tracks which were built to take away freshly caught herring, and is being pumped into destroyers. This photograph was taken in March 1910, when H.M.S. *Cossack* and H.M.S. *Tarter* came to Lowestoft to be bunkered with fuel oil, which was a cheaper alternative to coal. Likewise submarines came to be refuelled (below).

A naval amphibious aircraft (hydroplane) piloted by Commander Samson made a forced landing, on 12th July 1912, close to the beach between the Claremont and South Piers. He was on his way to Great Yarmouth when it developed a leaking valve. Crowds went to see it and boat trips took people for a closer look, as can be seen here to the left and right of the plane.

H.M.S. *Hearty*, seen here sailing out of the Inner Harbour, while her crew work on deck, was a 1,300 tons survey ship based in Lowestoft until 1901, when she was replaced by H.M.S. *Halcyon*. Her size was 212 x 30 ft, 4-3 pounder and built by Thomson of Dundee in 1885, she was used as a minesweeper during the war, which she survived to be sold in 1920. She carried out fisheries protection. During the years she was in Lowestoft her talented crew, the *Hearty Snowflakes*, did concerts to raise money for charity, including the local hospital.

H.M.S. *Jupiter*, seen off Lowestoft in June 1907, just before becoming part of the Home Fleet. This Majestic Class battleship was built at Thomson's Clydebank shipyard in 1895. During the First World War she was initially attached to the 7th Battle Squadron in the Channel Fleet, then went to Archangel as an icebreaker before patrolling the Red Sea and the Suez Canal. She was armed with four 12" guns, twelve 6" guns, sixteen 12 pounder guns, twelve 3 pounder guns and five torpedo tubes. Her speed was 16.5 knots. However, she was getting out of date and in 1916 was laid up before being scrapped in 1920.

On 14th September 1908 the fishing boat *Mercia* was returning to harbour when she was in collision with the warship H.M.S. *Leda*, a torpedo boat of 810 tons. *Mercia* sank in the harbour entrance. H.M.S. *Leda* can be seen in the distance on the right, as *Mercia* goes straight down.

H.M.S. *Halcyon*, here sailing out of the Inner Harbour, as the bridge swings shut behind her and passers by look on, was a surveillance gun boat of 107 tons which was based at Lowestoft from 1901, and patrolled the North Sea in the Great War. Her log book, during the war, indicates that most of the time she was in Lowestoft Harbour. There were mundane daily routines such as cleaning and painting ship, making and mending clothes, opening the ship to visitors, crew swiming lessons, and Division prayers. More dangerously, the crew also had to deal with a torpedo found by a fisherman in the North Sea, which they hoisted aboard to disarm.

Shortly after the war began, Halcyon was involved in the rescue of two ships' crews after a disaster into which the Court of Admiralty held an inquiry on 25th September 1914. In happier days, the steam drifter LT322 *Lindsell* could sail to sea with at least twenty people on board, including two ladies (as seen above). However on 3rd September 1914 at 11 a.m. she was sweeping for mines, when she struck one. The whole aft up to the funnel was destroyed.

Srak by mine

H.M.S. SPEEDY. SUNK BY MINE SEPT 3 1914

H.M.S. *Speedy* was on hand and immediately lowered both lifeboats and picked up six survivors. She is depicted here in Lowestoft Harbour, where she was based, her crew lining up on deck. Unfortunately at 11.15 a.m. *Speedy* also struck a mine. The whole of the after part of the ship was blown off as far as the ward room. The survivors were picked up from the stricken ship by the steam drifter *Sussex County*.

Lieutenant Commander Rutherford was the last to leave his ship, and as there was no boat to take him off, he walked down the side of the ship as she turned over, and jumped into the water from the keel as she sank. He was then picked up by one of the boats returning from the drifter where the remainder of the crew had been taken. *Sussex County* took the survivors to *Halcyon* at 12.25 and three quarters of an hour later the crew of *Speedy* were mustered for their monthly payment. However, it had been a sad day of loss. The Admiralty, and King and Queen sent a message of sympathy to the wives of those killed. Recipients included Mrs. Woodgate, widow of the late skipper Charles Woodgate, and Mrs. Bertie Sharman, of Carlton, whose husbands lost their lives through the blowing up of the Lowestoft steam drifter *Linsdell*. Mines were a great menace to the home fleet, as well as to the navy, but Lowestoft drifters were called on not only to sweep, but also to lay mines.

Another victim blown up by a mine was this poor old cod, which was blown onto the deck of the drifter *John and Norah*. One feature of the war was to be a darkly humorous interest in the unusual effects of high explosives, as the fact that this photograph was taken at all, shows.

The outbreak of the Great War produced many refugees. In September 1914 the government offered victims of war the hospitality of the British nation. Over a quarter of a million Belgian refugees came to Britain in the largest single refugee movement in British history. On October 15th at 11 a.m. Belgian refugees began arriving in Ostende smacks, flying the Belgian flag. 24 boats came that day. Here some are sailing into the harbour. On board were hundreds of men, women and children. One baby had died on the journey. Throngs of local people flocked down to the quay and cheered as the boats arrived. The poor folk on board responded feebly, some shouting *Vive L'Angleterre*. It was such a pitiful sight that many people cried without restraint. The crew of

HMS *Halcyon* were employed disembarking refugees. The first two or three Belgian boats to arrive were tied up alongside her, and people readily took nourishment of milk, biscuits and hot coffee from the sailors.

The flood gates of sympathy and charity opened spontaneously and by 9 p.m. nearly all the 1,150 refugees had been welcomed into private homes and institutions in Lowestoft. Others were accommodated at the skating rink in Kirkley, or went to Oulton Broad and Kessingland.

This Belgian children's home is thought to have been in the north end of the town and these are probably all the residents, with a matron.

A Belgian Relief Fund was set up. In December Mr. Alfred Eastty, who was sub-lieutenant Royal Naval Reserve on HMS *Victorian*, as well as a musical performer *The Banjo King*, sent a contribution of £7 to the fund.

The fishermen of Lowestoft were very experienced mariners, and bravely served at sea, clearing and laying mines, as well as acting as decoys. They would be trailed by a British submarine, in the hope that the smack would be attacked by a German U–boat, which the British could then engage and destroy. This work was very dangerous, as indeed was the continuing work of catching fish for the nation to eat. LT 513 trawler 1905 to 1918 *Active (left)*, built in Brixham, Devon was sunk on 6th June 1918 by U-boat gunfire five miles from Smith's Knoll Spar buoy. Attacks by U-Boats on our trade routes and on our fishermen reached a peak in August 1915, and minelaying by submarines increased in the south of the North Sea. Many fishing smacks were stopped and captured by German submarines. Sometimes they would be set on fire, but mostly had timed bombs placed on them and sunk. During August, thirty Lowestoft smacks were destroyed, and anxiety grew for the fish supply.

Meantime air attack had increased and continual Zeppelin raids were disturbing the east coast. Special measures were taken to protect the fishing fleet, and the Admiralty requisitioned many fishing boats, which were used as patrol boats and minesweepers.

The smack, in the lower picture, next to a naval vessel, may be being repaired as a white plank of wood is being replaced, or it may be having its name changed. The wooden float bears the letters L W W H R. The drifters' names were frequently changed to avoid detection. The boats would be painted over in the harbour and sent to sea again under a different name. These boats were exposed to attack from the small U-boats which operated out of Zeebrugge.

Four of them, the *G and E, Pet, Glory and Inverlyon* were armed with 3 pounders. Corbett in his book *The Official History of the War- Naval Operations* states: *By the end of the month all of them, except the Glory, had been in action with a U boat, and claimed to have destroyed her by gun fire. The three claims were allowed, but only one, the destruction of UB4 by the Inverlyon, was ever verified.*

The Lowestoft Maritime Museum holds the following information about these boats and the fate of the U-boats: 11th August 1915, the armed trawler G and E, LT649, [skipper Moxey], sank UB4 near Smith's Knoll by gunfire. The submarine had just sunk some Lowestoft smacks and came at the G and E intending to sink her, but received 4 shots into his hull in one minute, which sent him to the bottom. Skipper Moxey picked up the flagpole and German Ensign on the spot where the U-Boat sank.

15th August 1915, the armed smack Inverlyon, LT687, [skipper Tom Phillips DSM] sank a U-Boat by gunfire 4 miles N by E of Smith's Knoll Spar Buoy. The skipper was awarded £1,000 and the DSM. The German Officer shut the conning tower and left his men to their fate on the whale back when the Inverlyon opened fire. [Skipper Phillips was later taken prisoner in April 1916.]

23rd August 1915, the armed smack Pet, LT 560, [skipper Moore], sank a U Boat by gunfire off Smith's Knoll, after a 2 hour fight. The U-Boat had sunk several unarmed Lowestoft smacks and attacked the Pet, intending to sink her. Skipper Moore was awarded £1,000 by the Admiralty.

Despite these successes, the *Lowestoft Journal* reported in August 1915 that more smacks had been sunk. The crews of the trawlers *Admiral, George Crabbe, Illustrious, Palm, Trevonce* and *Welcome, Esperance, Leader, Ocean's Gift* and *George Borrow* were landed, all the vessels having been bombed.

The *Superb* LT 938 was a wooden sailing trawler. In the First World War she was hired by the Admiralty to be used as a fighting boat. She was captured by a submarine on 13th November 1916, 5 miles NE by E from Smith's Knoll Spar buoy, and sunk by gunfire from the U-boat. Built in only 1902, she had a short and unlucky life as she had previously sunk in the harbour entrance on 28th October 1912, after being struck by the steam drifter *Sussex County*. She was raised on the 6th November by divers from H.M.S. *Leda*, who patched her up. Here she is being pumped out.

It is hard to overstate the bravery of the Lowestoft fishermen, or the dangers they faced. The story of one of Lowestoft's most gallant men, Tom Crisp, skipper of the smack *Nelson*, was told in the House of Commons by the Prime Minister, Lloyd George, when he was referring to the splendid service given by fishermen in the war. While out fishing, the *Nelson* was fired on by a German submarine, which kept well out of range of the *Nelson's* little 3 pounder gun. The *Nelson's* gunner kept up a steady reply, as they tried to close the distance from the U-boat. However the enemy's seventh shell found its target, hitting Tom Crisp, and going straight through the smack. Despite his terrible, fatal injuries, Tom remained conscious and told his son to send this message: *Nelson being attacked by submarine. Skipper killed. Send assistance at once.* Only five rounds of ammunition were left for the 3 pounder, but the *Nelson* was sinking. The skipper ordered the ship's books to be thrown overboard so the Germans couldn't get them, and then the crew prepared to abandon ship. Tom said goodbye to his son, being too badly injured to be moved, and he insisted they save themselves. As the crew climbed into the small boat, Tom Crisp went down with his ship. Such was his heroism that Tom Crisp was posthumously awarded the Victoria Cross.

The German army and navy used Zeppelins as bombers during the First World War. Zeppelins were between 150 and 160 metres long, and could travel up to 49 miles per hour, being powered by three Maybach motors of about 400 to 550 horse power. They had volumes of 22,000-25,000 cubic capacity, which enabled them to carry loads of around 20,000lbs. This allowed them to carry more bombs and guns than an aeroplane. Their weakness, however, was that they were very vulnerable to gunfire.

They were also used in reconnaissance over the North Sea. Their night time raids were intended to only target military sites, but many bombs fell randomly in East Anglia after blackout became widespread. The first raid involving civilian life was in January 1915, when 24 high explosive bombs were dropped on Great Yarmouth, Sheringham, King's Lynn and surrounding villages. A further nineteen attacks took place in 1915. Lowestoft was one of the targets.

At 1.15 a.m. on the morning of 16th April 1915, a hooter sounded at the Lowestoft Destruction Centre to wake everyone up. Many were already awake, having slept downstairs, as they thought a Zeppelin raid was imminent. The loud whirring noise of the Zeppelin could be heard as it made its way over the North Sea on that windless, starlit night. Suddenly the sky was lit up by a large flare, as three loud explosions were heard. At 1.30 a.m. the Zeppelin headed back across the sea, and the whirring gradually grew fainter as it disappeared into the distance. The people of Lowestoft calmly came outside to view the damage. Bevan Street shop windows were shattered, and Clapham Road was covered with glass. The Suffolk Hotel also had broken windows. The tram track in Denmark Road felt hot and was splattered with a coloured liquid.

The correspondent for the 1915 Great Eastern Railway magazine made this observation about East Anglia: *Quite a number of bombs have now evidently been thrown at GER railway stations.* This was so at Lowestoft when not only a carriage body was damaged but also the property round about.

The most damage in Denmark Road occurred at four houses, including No. 46 where Mr. and Mrs. Fitt lived, and No. 52 where Mrs. Mobb lived. No. 50 was unoccupied at the time. The windows of this house in Denmark Road were shattered, but it looks, from the cart in the foreground, as if builders have already arrived to make good the damage. A number of mothers or nurses are eagerly discussing the matter.

ZEPPELIN RAID ON LOWESTOFT APR 16.1915
HOLE MADE BY BOMB IN DENMARK RD.

C METCALF
LOWESTOFT

15
HOLE MADE BY ZEPPELIN BOMB IN DENMARK RD. LOWESTOFT APR 16.1915

C METCALF.
LOWESTOFT.

Mr. and Mrs. Pratt lived at No. 48, and they had a hole four feet deep in their back garden only ten feet from the house. Many people, military and civilian, came along to pose in the crater, while C. Metcalfe of Lowestoft took the photos from various different angles.

Major Chauncy, an eyewitness said: *In the back yard of one house I saw a hole large enough to bury a horse, and the back wall of a house practically destroyed. The whole house was so shaken that it was beyond repair, but the tenant, his wife and children who were sleeping in the house miraculously managed to escape unscathed. Such is war upon fortified towns.*

Outbuildings in Denmark Road were wrecked, as were the stables nearby. Major Chauncy said: *The bomb fell on some stables, blew in the windows and killed two horses, besides wounding others. The horses were stabled facing the windows. Poor brutes, struck down in the darkness with no knowledge that a mighty empire wrought three years to your destruction!*

The bomb made a large hole in the ground and shattered several lorries standing by. The force with which the missiles were scattered is evidenced by the fact that pieces cut through the stout lorry tyres as though they had been paper; a piece of wood, too, was blown right through the wall of a house. Nearly all the windows in the adjacent road were broken by the shock, and the fact that none of the people sleeping in front of the houses was injured is no doubt due to the stables intervening between the houses and the bomb.

Right: The death toll of this Zeppelin raid amounted to two horses and one sparrow. Evidently the body of the unfortunate sparrow was recovered soon enough for H. Jenkins to photograph it. It says something about the slightly morbid fascination people had for bomb damage that this was considered a saleable postcard.

Lowesestoft Air Raid APRIL 15 191
Victims of German Frightfullness
2 HORSE 1 SPARROW
H. JENKINS LOWESTOFT

Several premises in Commercial Road had been hit. Messrs. R. & J. Latten, a timber merchants, was one of them. A naval crew moored alongside kept the fire in check, together with marines and soldiers, until the fire brigade arrived in the motor fire engine. Mr. L. W. Abbott, who lived on the premises, had a narrow escape.

R. & J. LATTEN LTD TIMBER YARD
ZEPPELIN RAID APRIL 1915

Left: The South Pier was used to accommodate naval men, and was hit in this raid. No-one was hurt and the damage, broken railings and superficial holes, soon repaired. The pavilion continued in use until World War Two, when it was so severely bombed that it had to be demolished.

This was not the only raid over East Anglia. Rider Haggard wrote in his private diaries of some of them. His large house on the cliff, Kessingland Grange, was taken over by the military and he had to move out. He spent some time at Ditchingham near Bungay. On 10th August 1915 he wrote: *Last night about 10.30 we heard the heavy detonation of bombs from the direction of the coast, so heavy that windows shook and clocks were stopped at the Lodge. All I can get from railway guards, PO officials etc is that the Zeppelins attacked the front at Lowestoft, killing soldiers and others.* The following day he went to Lowestoft and saw the terrible damage done by the bombs, the wrecked houses, the shattered windows, the bed from which a poor girl had been hurled and killed.

Later in the month, Lowestoft was attacked again. He wrote on 15th August: *Yesterday I motored to Southwold and Lowestoft. Southwold is deserted, no one on the beach, except a few soldiers and their girls. Barbed wire defences everywhere, also trenches and sandbags, though what the use of them is I do not know, as they look to me as though they could easily be turned by an invading force taking advantage of the deep water, to land here, if it can.*
At Lowestoft I saw the bomb-shattered houses. In one of them a poor old landlady sat disconsolate by her broken window – a melancholy sight. The proprietor of the tea-shop told me she was shutting up her place and going away.

The raids continued throughout the war. Charles Dyer, a picture frame maker of Gt Yarmouth wrote a letter, which was censored on 8th August 1916 and returned: *We had a great German air raid two nights ago. Those devils were over Yarmouth for the best part of three hours. Hilda and I went out to see what could be seen. It was a dark black night, and to hear these fearful things overhead and to know that at any moment a bomb may drop and shatter one into jelly is not a pleasant feeling by any means. Twice there was a Zeppelin directly over our heads. They kick up a fearful row, for all the world like an express train in the sky. Fortunately they were so high up and our town is always plunged into such profound darkness that they were in ignorance of the fact that they were right over our town hall and quay several times. Not one bomb was dropped in Yarmouth, but we heard them in all directions in the surrounding country. The very pavement shook with the shock though the bomb was miles away. There were over 100 bombs dropped in the vicinity. However, we're still alive thank God.*

Rider Haggard gave his account of 3rd September 1916: *We had a terrible time last night Zeppelins were about. A bomb exploded quite near, about 200 yards from the house. There followed a veritable rain of them. By the goodness of God they missed both this house, over which the zeppelin was hanging, and the cottages. It was hellish – the whirr of the machine above, the fearful boom of the bombs, and the spawning shells, and we sat for hours in the cellar.*

Remains of a German bomb dropped in the 16 April raid.

On 17th June 1917, six Zeppelins were detailed for a raid on London, but two could not leave their sheds because of strong wind, and two turned back with engine failure. Only L42 and L48 pressed on. The L48 was originally the LZ95 (L= luft, German for air, and Z= Zeppelin). It was the 95th Zeppelin built by the Von Zeppelin company. The German navy renamed it L48 when it was launched on 22nd May 1917. She was one of the latest types and could climb higher, having a volume of 55,800 square metres and being 196.5 metres long. The aluminium framework was divided into compartments and was capable of carrying a crew of 40.

L48 dropped bombs around the Harwich area and started to head back east. Searchlights spotted her and as soon as she was visible to enemy aircraft, some British home defence pilots followed. They were Lieutenant F. D. Holder (right) of East Kent

Regiment and Royal Flying Corps, with Sergeant S. Ashby (left) his gunner, flying an FE2b B401, and Lieutenant E. W. Clarke, flying a BE2c (A8896), Captain R.H.M.S. Saundby in DH2 A5058, all from the Armament Experimental Station at Orfordness, and Lieutenant P Watkins in BE12 6610 from 37 (HD) Squadron (A Flight) at Goldhanger.

Holder was at 14,200 feet, well below the L48, and he had difficulty in climbing and following her erratic course at the same time. Both Holder and Ashby opened fire, but then Holder's gun jammed and would not clear. As the Zeppelin descended Holder followed and Ashby was able to continue firing. 30 rounds were fired from the 5th drum before Ashby's Lewis gun jammed. As Holder turned away for him to clear it, the Zeppelin began to fall in flames. At around 2.30 a.m. the Zeppelin crashed in flames into a field at Holly Tree Farm, Theberton, Suffolk.

It was decided that, due to the small aircraft windows and the way in which the planes had to dart about, it was impossible for pilots to see the other pilots firing. So it was not certain who actually fired the shot that caused the flames. The War Office awarded credit to Watkins, but decided that it was a shared victory. The King conferred the Military Cross for conspicuous gallantry on attacking and destroying an enemy airship on the pilots and gunners in both planes.

The German military recorded *One reconnaissance mission successful. As part of an attempted attack on London with three others became lost and was then intercepted and destroyed by British fighters over sea near Great Yarmouth, 17th June 1917, crashing near Leiston, two survivors.*

The other Zeppelin, L42, was pursued out to sea close to Lowestoft.

The Graf Zeppelin over Lowestoft August 1931. but people remembered the ones that came during the war.

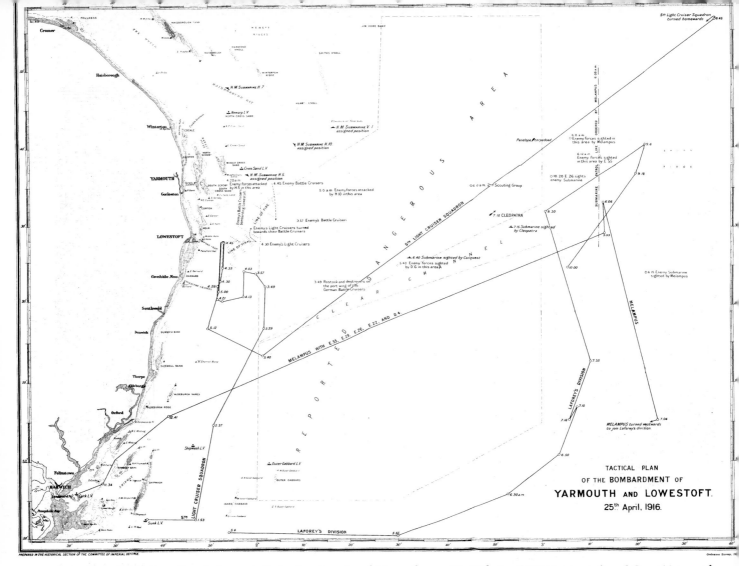

TACTICAL PLAN
OF THE BOMBARDMENT OF
YARMOUTH AND LOWESTOFT.
25th April, 1916.

As well as attacks from the air, Lowestoft also faced onslaught from the sea. On 25th April 1916 Lowestoft and Great Yarmouth were bombarded by a squadron of German ships. Just after 4 a.m. Lowestoft was woken up by a loud boom, which was followed by a quick succession of deafening explosions, as shells were fired from ships. These crashed into the town or went screaming overhead into the countryside beyond, injuring cattle.

An Admiralty report on this action says that the Germans knew their fleet was no match for the Royal Navy, and the raid was one of several such sorties mounted with the idea of drawing ships from the British fleet into waters close to the German coast where they could be attacked. The *Lutzow* and *Derfflinger* were the only warships to shell the town. The *Lutzow* fired eighteen 12 inch, 45 x 5.9 inch shells, and the *Derfflinger*, sixteen 12 inch and 32 x 9 inch shells. The brief engagement was broken off with the arrival of the Harwich force. One of the British light cruisers, *Conquest*, hit the German flagship *Seydlitz*, killing 25 of her crew and seriously wounding thirteen others. Two German submarines were also lost in the operation, while two British ships were damaged and a submarine lost.

People went to the seafront to watch the battle at sea with the squadron of big ships stretching right across the horizon from north to south. Flashes of incessant firing could be seen through binoculars and great fountains of water sprang up as shells struck the water. As soon as the British ships engaged in battle, the German ships went out to sea at great speed. The low rumbling of gun fire could still be heard for a further hour or so.

This *Tactile Plan of the Bombardment of Yarmouth and Lowestoft 25th April 1916,* printed in 1922, by the Committee of Imperial Defence (Historical Section), shows the line up of the ships off Lowestoft at the time of the bombardment. At 3.57 a.m. the enemy's battle cruisers were in place and started to bombard Lowestoft with shells. British ships hurried towards the scene. The submarine H5 attacked the enemy forces at 4.20 a.m. The British 5th Light Cruiser Squadron was on its way up from Harwich and was off Covehithe. They went landside of the Germans and were at Lowestoft at 4.45 a.m., where they exchanged fire with the enemy. At 5 a.m. submarine H 10 attacked the enemy forces from the seaward side, and the German flotilla fled to sea. The 5th Light Squadron headed out to sea in pursuit to join HMS *Melumpus* which had been on patrol throughout the night with 5 submarines. Various German submarines were sighted, and one torpedoed the British *Penelope*, blowing away her rudder and wrecking her steering gear, although she could still steam at twenty knots.

Above: Such was the fascination with shells that when this shell landed in Lighthouse Score, and failed to explode, Happy Welham quickly swept it into his garden, charging the public to look at it, until the authorities arrived. As this picture shows, even when the soldiers put the shell under guard, plenty of people were very keen to look at it and be photographed close to it.

Left: The firefight at sea left shells littered over the sea bed, which were from time to time trawled up and of course photographed being held by the lucky finder.

Although the firing at Lowestoft only lasted fifteen to twenty minutes much damage was done to property. 200 houses, a convalescent home, swimming baths, shops and the pier were damaged. Damage to property spread right across town. There were many stories of near death experiences, but considering the amount of damage to buildings there was very little harm done to people, many of the houses being empty at the time. Three lives were lost in Sandringham Road and three people were injured in the convalescent home. The strong, indignant feeling of local people was that Lowestoft was an open town full of non-combatants who were being murdered in their sleep (although it was of course also an important naval base). An inquest was held on the four dead, who were, Mr. W. T. Holies from Westcliffe, Essex, Ann E. Davy age 21, Sidney H. Davy age sixteen, and baby Robert Mumford aged eight months.

BOMBARDMENT of LOWESTOFT APRIL 25 16. KENT R?
SHELL WENT THROUGH 13 HOUSES TAKEN OUT of BEDROOM UNEXPLODED
NOBODY KILLED OR INJOURED MANY NARROW ESCAPES.
12 inch SHELL WEIGHED 8 cwt 96 lbs. H.JENKIN §

In Kent Road a twelve inch shell travelled through thirteen houses, knocking out bay windows and weakening the brick work. It came to rest in a cupboard but still did not go off. Miraculously nobody was killed or injured and it was dismantled by the Royal Navy, along with six other such shells from the bombardment.

London Road South received a lot of damage. Here the corner shop on the left was all but demolished, and has been cordoned off with barrels and a plank of wood, which a soldier is standing by. People carried on their daily lives, walking or riding bikes along the street staring in amazement at the destruction. While a horse and cart is passing by, the trams could not run due to the trolley wires being damaged. Damage was done upstairs at No. 161, London Road South, which belonged to Durrant and Son, fruit and vegetable growers. Next door to it was the Ironmongers, Reffell and Co., and then the photographer's shop, which took a hit to the roof. Many business were struck by shells, including a fancy drapers, a tobacconist's shop and a provision merchants on the corner.

Uniformed men standing guard outside a house in St. Leonards Road where the roof and front bedroom had collapsed.

A house in Cleveland Road after the bombardment. All in all, houses suffered in Yarmouth Road, Sandringham Road, Clemence Street, Cleveland Road, Windsor Road, London Road South, The Esplanade, Norwich Road, Kirkley Run, Kent Road, St. Leonards Road and Carlton Road. The total damage was estimated to be £25,000.

These four new houses had only recently been built in Kirkley Run when two of them were destroyed by shells.

Two soldiers with a little family outside their badly damaged home in Clemence Street. While the soldiers are smiling, the lady looks particularly unimpressed.

Sandringham Road where three lives were lost.

Lowestoft Convalescent Home in 1911. In the course of the raid three people were injured here.

The convalescent home was given by Mr. William Birkbeck, one of the leading figures of Barclays Bank, and opened in 1877. It had close links with the bank and was mainly maintained through voluntary contributions. Before the Second World War between 400 and 500 benefited there yearly. In World War Two it was used as a Church Army hostel and housed naval men.

A house on the esplanade totally destroyed. This was one of the spectacular houses built by Peto along the promenade, and was right in the firing line. Only a very few of the row now remain.

After four years of death and danger at sea and at home, Lowestoft had peace once more. One of the events which celebrated the end of the war was the opening of this holiday centre for convalescent ex-servicemen in 1919.

Funds were raised locally as well as in other parts of the country, in order to buy this house, on Kirkley Cliff, which had once been owned by the Colman mustard family of Norwich.

Lord Kitchener of Khartoum, was a national hero in the 1890s after the Battle of Omdurman, near Khartoum and became Secretary of State for War at the outbreak of World War 1. His call for volunteers was answered by a great number of recruits but he lost his life in 1916 on the cruiser *Hampshire*, when it was sunk west of the Orkneys. His high profile with the public brought about many projects as memorials to his life, and the scheme for this house was put forward before the Armistice in 1918.

There was a grand opening ceremony on 7th August 1919, commencing with a public meeting at the Hippodrome, Lowestoft. The Lowestoft Federation Band played, under Bandmaster Alger, and led the procession to the centre for the opening ceremony. There was a guard of honour of men who had served at Mons, under ex-sergeant Munnings. It was opened by General Sir Henry Horne, a friend of Lord Kitchener, on whose staff he had served in Gallipoli. Tea was taken on the lawn, which later became a putting green.

Today the centre still provides subsidised holidays for ex-servicemen, and is a registered charity funded by sponsorship from service charities and by donations from visitors and the people of Lowestoft.

These sailors are recovering from war injuries at hospital. Injured sailors from HMS *Halcyon* were sent to Gunton sick quarters. Note the very patriotic dog.